FRANKLIN DELANO ROOSEVELT

FRANKLIN DELANO ROOSEVELT

Fred L. Israel

Burke Publishing Company Limited
LONDON ∗ TORONTO ∗ NEW YORK

First published in the United States of America 1985
© 1985 by Chelsea House Publishers,
a division of Chelsea House Communications, Inc. All rights reserved.
Introduction © Arthur M. Schlesinger Jr. 1985
This edition first published 1988
New material in this edition © Burke Publishing Company 1988

ACKNOWLEDGEMENTS
The Author and Publishers are grateful to the following organizations for
permission to reproduce copyright illustrations in this book:
    AP/Wide World Photos, The Bettmann Archive, The Franklin Delano
    Roosevelt Library and UPI/Bettmann Newsphotos.

CIP data
Israel, Fred L.
    Franklin Delano Roosevelt. —(World leaders).
    1. United States. Roosevelt, Franklin D.
    (Franklin Delano), *1882–1945*, Biographies
    I. Title   II. Series
    973.917'092'4

ISBN 0 222 01244 7 Hardbound
ISBN 0 222 01245 5 Paperback

Burke Publishing Company Limited
Pegasus House, 116–120 Golden Lane, London EC1Y 0TL, England
Printed in England by Purnell Book Production Limited.

CONTENTS

WORLD LEADERS   PAST AND PRESENT

KONRAD ADENAUER
ALEXANDER THE GREAT
MARK ANTONY
KING ARTHUR
KEMAL ATATÜRK
CLEMENT ATTLEE
MENACHEM BEGIN
DAVID BEN GURION
BISMARCK
LÉON BLUM
SÍMON BOLÍVAR
CESARE BORGIA
WILLY BRANDT
LEONID BREZHNEV
JULIUS CEASAR
CALVIN
FIDEL CASTRO
CATHERINE THE GREAT
CHARLEMAGNE
CHIANG KAI-SHEK
CHOU EN-LAI
WINSTON CHURCHILL
CLEMENCEAU
CLEOPATRA
CORTES
CROMWELL
DANTON
CHARLES DE GAULLE
DE VALERA
DISRAELI
DWIGHT D. EISENHOWER
ELEANOR OF AQUITAINE
QUEEN ELIZABETH I

FERDINAND AND ISABELLA
FRANCO
FREDERICK THE GREAT
INDIRA GANDHI
MOHANDAS K. GANDHI
GARIBALDI
GENGHIS KHAN
GLADSTONE
DAG HAMMARSKJÖLD
HENRY VIII
HENRY OF NAVARRE
HINDENBURG
ADOLF HITLER
HO CHI MINH
KING HUSSEIN
IVAN THE TERRIBLE
ANDREW JACKSON
THOMAS JEFFERSON
JOAN OF ARC
POPE JOHN XXIII
LYNDON JOHNSON
BENITO JUÁREZ
JOHN F. KENNEDY
JOMO KENYATTA
AYATOLLAH KHOMEINI
NIKITA KHRUSHCHEV
MARTIN LUTHER KING
HENRY KISSINGER
VLADIMIR LENIN
ABRAHAM LINCOLN
LLOYD GEORGE
LOUIS XIV
MARTIN LUTHER
JUDAS MACCABEUS

MAO TSE TUNG
MARY, QUEEN OF SCOTS
GOLDA MEIR
METTERNICH
BENITO MUSSOLINI
NAPOLEON
JAMAL NASSER
JAWALHARLAL NEHRU
NERO
NICHOLAS II
RICHARD NIXON
KWAME NKRUMAH
PERICLES
JUAN PERÓN
MUAMMAR QADDAFI
ROBESPIERRE
ELEANOR ROOSEVELT
FRANKLIN D. ROOSEVELT
THEODORE ROOSEVELT
ANWAR SADAT
SUN YAT-SEN
JOSEPH STALIN
TAMERLANE
MARGARET THATCHER
IOSIF TITO
LEON TROTSKY
PIERRE TRUDEAU
HARRY S. TRUMAN
QUEEN VICTORIA
GEORGE WASHINGTON
CHAIM WEIZMANN
WOODROW WILSON
XERXES

LEADERSHIP, it may be said, is really what makes the world go round. Love no doubt smooths the passage; but love is a private transaction between consenting adults. Leadership is a public transaction with history. The idea of leadership affirms the capacity of individuals to move, inspire and mobilize masses of people so that they act together in pursuit of an end. Sometimes leadership serves good purposes, sometimes bad; but whether the end is benign or evil, great leaders are those men and women who leave their personal stamp on history.

Now, the very concept of leadership implies the proposition that individuals can make a difference. This proposition has never been universally accepted. From classical times to the present day, eminent thinkers have regarded individuals as no more than the agents and pawns of larger forces, whether the gods and goddesses of the ancient world or, in the modern era, race, class, nation, the dialectic, the will of the people, the spirit of the times, history itself. Against such forces, the individual dwindles into insignificance.

So contends the thesis of historical determinism. Tolstoy's great novel *War and Peace* offers a famous statement of the case. Why, Tolstoy asked, did millions of men in the Napoleonic wars, denying their human feelings and their common sense, move back and forth across Europe slaughtering their fellows? "The war," Tolstoy answered, "was bound to happen simply because it was bound to happen." All prior history predetermined it. As for leaders, they, Tolstoy said, "are but the labels that serve to give a name to an end and, like labels, they have the least possible connection with the event." The greater the leader, "the more conspicuous the inevitability and the predestination of every act he commits." The leader, said Tolstoy, is "the slave of history".

Determinism takes many forms. Marxism is the determinism of class, Nazism the determinism of race. But the idea of men and women as the slaves of history runs athwart the deepest human instincts. Rigid determinism abolishes the idea of human freedom—the assumption of free choice that underlies every move we make, every word we speak, every thought we think. It abolishes the idea of human responsibility, since it is manifestly unfair to reward or punish people for actions that are by definition beyond their control. No one can live consistently by any deterministic creed. The Marxist states prove this themselves by their extreme susceptibility to the cult of leadership.

More than that, history refutes the idea that individuals make no difference. In December 1931 a British politician crossing Park Avenue in New York City between 76th and 77th Streets around ten-thirty at night looked in the wrong direction and was knocked down by a speeding car—a moment, he later recalled, of a man aghast, a world aglare: "I do not understand why I was not broken like an eggshell or squashed like a gooseberry." Fourteen months later an American politician, sitting in an open car in Miami, Florida, was fired on by an assassin; the man beside him was hit. Those who believe that individuals make no difference to history might well ponder whether the next two decades would have been the same, had Mario Contasini's car killed Winston Churchill in 1931 and had Giuseppe Zangara's bullet killed Franklin Roosevelt in 1933. Suppose, in addition, that Adolf Hitler had been killed in the street fighting during the Munich *Putsch* of 1923 and that Lenin had died of typhus during the First World War. What would the 20th century be like now?

For better or for worse, individuals do make a difference. "The notion that a people can run itself and its affairs anonymously," wrote the philosopher William James, "is now well known to be the silliest of absurdities. Mankind does nothing save through initiatives on the part of inventors, great or small, and imitation by the rest of us—these are the sole factors in human progress. Individuals of genius show the way, and set the patterns, which common people then adopt and follow."

Leadership, James suggests, means leadership in thought as well as in action. In the long run, leaders in thought may well make the greater difference to the world. But, as Woodrow Wilson once said, "Those only are leaders of men, in the general eye, who lead in action . . . It is at their hands that new thought gets its translation into the crude language of deeds." Leaders in thought often invent in solitude and obscurity, leaving to later generations the tasks of imitation. Leaders in action—the leaders portrayed in this series—have to be effective in their own time.

And they cannot be effective by themselves. They must act in response to the rhythms of their age. Their genius must be adapted, in a phrase of William James's, "to the receptivities of the moment". Leaders are useless without followers. "There goes the mob," said the French politician hearing a clamour in the streets. "I am their leader. I must follow them." Great leaders turn the inchoate emotions of the mob to purposes of their own. They seize on the opportunities of their time, the hopes, fears, frustrations, crises, potentialities. They succeed when events have prepared the way for them, when the community is waiting to be aroused, when they can provide the clarifying and organizing ideas. Leadership ignites the circuit between the individual and the mass and thereby alters history. It may alter history for better or for worse. Leaders have been responsible for the most extravagant follies and most monstrous crimes that have beset suffering humanity. They have also been vital in such gains as humanity has made in individual freedom, religious and racial tolerance, social justice and respect for human rights.

There is no sure way to tell in advance who is going to lead for good and who for evil. But a glance at the gallery of men and women in *World Leaders—Past and Present* suggests some useful tests.

One test is this: do leaders lead by force or by persuasion? By command or by consent? Through most of history leadership was exercised by the divine right of authority. The duty of followers was to defer and to obey. *"Their's not to reason why,/Their's but to do and die."* On occasion, as with the so-called "enlightened despots" of the 18th century in Europe, absolutist leadership was animated by humane purposes. More often, absolutism nourished the passion for domination, land, gold and conquest and resulted in tyranny.

The great revolution of modern times has been the revolution of equality. The idea that all people should be equal in their legal condition has undermined the old structures of authority, hierarchy and deference. The revolution of equality has had two contrary effects on the nature of leadership. For equality, as Alexis de Tocqueville pointed out in his great study *Democracy in America,* might mean equality in servitude as well as equality in freedom.

"I know of only two methods of establishing equality in the political world," Tocqueville wrote. "Rights must be given to every citizen, or none at all to anyone . . . save one, who is the master of all." There was no middle ground "between the sovereignty of all and the absolute power of one man". In his astonishing prediction of 20th-century totalitarian dictatorship, Tocqueville explained how the revolution of equality could lead to the *Führerprinzip* and more terrible absolutism than the world had ever known.

But when rights are given to every citizen and the sovereignty of all is established, the problem of leadership takes a new form, becomes more exacting than ever before. It is easy to issue commands and enforce them by the rope and the stake, the concentration camp and the *gulag.* It is much harder to use argument and achievement to overcome opposition and win consent. The Founding Fathers of the United States understood the difficulty. They believed that history had given them the opportunity to decide, as Alexander Hamilton wrote in the first Federalist Paper, whether men are indeed capable of basing government on "reflection and choice, or whether they are forever destined to depend . . . on accident and force."

Government by reflection and choice called for a new style of leadership and a new quality of followership. It required leaders to be responsive to popular concerns, and it required followers to be active and informed participants in the process. Democracy does not eliminate emotion from politics; sometimes it fosters demagogy; but it is confident that, as the greatest of democratic leaders put it, you cannot fool all of the people all of the time. It measures leadership by results and retires those who overreach or falter or fail.

It is true that in the long run despots are measured by results too. But they can postpone the day of judgement, sometimes indefinitely, and in the meantime they can do infinite harm. It is also true that democracy is no guarantee of virtue and intelligence in government, for the voice of the people is not necessarily the voice of God. But democracy, by assuring the rights of opposition, offers built-in resistance to the evils inherent in absolutism. As the theologian Reinhold Niebuhr summed it up, "Man's capacity for justice makes democracy possible, but man's inclination to injustice makes democracy necessary."

A second test for leadership is the end for which power is sought. When leaders have as their goal the supremacy of a master race or the promotion of totalitarian revolution or the acquisition and exploitation of colonies or the protection of greed and privilege or the preservation of personal power, it is likely that their leadership will do little to advance the cause of humanity. When their goal is the abolition of slavery, the liberation of women, the enlargement of opportunity for the poor and powerless, the extension of equal rights to racial minorities, the defence of the freedoms of expression and opposition, it is likely that their leadership will increase the sum of human liberty and welfare.

Leaders have done great harm to the world. They have also conferred great benefits. You will find both sorts in this series. Even "good" leaders must be regarded with a certain wariness. Leaders are not demigods; they put on their trousers one leg after another just like ordinary mortals. No leader is infallible, and every leader needs to be reminded of this at regular intervals. Irreverence irritates leaders but is their salvation. Unquestioning submission corrupts leaders and demeans followers. Making a cult of a leader is always a mistake. Fortunately hero worship generates its own antidote. "Every hero," said Emerson, "becomes a bore at last."

The signal benefit the great leaders confer is to embolden the rest of us to live according to our own best selves, to be active, insistent, and resolute in affirming our own sense of things. For great leaders attest to the reality of human freedom against the supposed inevitabilities of history. And they attest to the wisdom and power that may lie within the most unlikely of us, which is why Abraham Lincoln remains the supreme example of great leadership. A great leader, said Emerson, exhibits new possibilities to all humanity. "We feed on genius . . . Great men exist that there may be greater men."

Great leaders, in short, justify themselves by emancipating and empowering their followers. So humanity struggles to master its destiny, remembering with Alexis de Tocqueville: "It is true that around every man a fatal circle is traced beyond which he cannot pass; but within the wide verge of that circle he is powerful and free; as it is with man, so with communities."

ARTHUR M. SCHLESINGER JR.
New York

Author's Preface_____

F ranklin D. Roosevelt ranks as one of the greatest presidents in American history. His presidential administrations (1933–1945) coped with two of the most important events of the 20th century—the Great Depression and World War II. In handling these momentous problems, Roosevelt became a personal, larger-than-life hero to millions—a president who could do no wrong. Likewise, because of the fundamental changes to the nation's economy caused by his policies, millions of others came to hate "that man in the White House". Nevertheless, even his detractors must agree that Franklin D. Roosevelt indeed left an indelible mark on American history.

Roosevelt died in office on 12 April 1945, less than three months after his inauguration for an unprecendented fourth term. Unlike presidents Truman, Eisenhower, Johnson, Nixon, Ford, and Carter, Roosevelt wrote no memoirs, no autobiography, no personal recollection of his inner feelings and motivations. We have excellent documentation of Roosevelt's life as material about him has been made public far more rapidly than with other presidents. But, despite collections of letters; the reminiscences of family, friends, and associates; the writings by so many who were associated with Roosevelt in every conceivable way; and despite the many thoughtful studies of his life and of his presidency, Roosevelt the man still remains elusive. Once a young reporter asked President Roosevelt about his philosophy:

"Mr. President, are you a Communist?"
"No."

"Are you a capitalist?"

"No."

"Are you a Socialist?"

"No!" he said, with a look of surprise, as if he wondered about what he was being cross-examined.

The young man said, "Well, what is your philosophy, then?"

"Philosophy?" asked the president, puzzled. "Philosophy? I am a Christian and a Democrat. That's all."

Perhaps unknowingly, Roosevelt had thus given a most accurate description of himself. Never a prisoner of ideology, Roosevelt aimed instead for flexibility—he was willing to make changes and was fully prepared to discard policies and programmes when necessary. Above all, though, Roosevelt projected an image of self-confidence. He radiated a feeling of concern for the less fortunate and seemed genuinely interested in improving people's lives. To those closest to him during the White House years, he was always charming, impressive, and an inexhaustible source of energy and power.

Although, due to illness, Roosevelt lost the use of his legs at age 39, he never allowed himself to indulge in self-pity. He chose instead to face all the obstacles which confronted the people who had placed their trust in him. While others lacked the courage to depart from the old, accepted rules of American politics, Roosevelt repeatedly took unprecendented risks. His dynamic leadership never ceased to convey a sense of trust, of assurance, and of bravery.

1

A Young Patrician

Franklin Delano Roosevelt was born at his family home, Springwood, in Hyde Park, New York, on 30 January 1882. Hyde Park is a small village overlooking the Hudson River about 80 miles from New York City and five miles north of the town of Poughkeepsie. By the time of Franklin's birth, several generations of Roosevelts had made their homes along the beautiful Hudson River valley. It is thought that the first Roosevelt in America came from Holland around 1648.

Franklin's father, James Roosevelt, had purchased Springwood and over the years had increased his land holdings to more than 1,000 acres. From the porch of this stately home was a magnificent view of the river valley and the Catskill Mountains beyond. Herds of cattle grazed the land, and rolling hills, fields of grain, greenhouses, grape arbours, flowering gardens, goats, dogs, and stables for riding horses and racing trotters filled the panorama. Indeed, Franklin was born to a wealthy family—a family that had enjoyed immense privilege for many generations, a family that was far removed from the great world of the underprivileged.

Franklin D. Roosevelt (1882–1945) spent his first 14 years with his parents at Springwood, their Hyde Park, N.Y., estate or travelling with them abroad. Except for six weeks at a school in Germany and tutoring at home in such subjects as Latin, French, German, and history, his serious academic training did not begin until he entered Groton School at the age of fourteen.

Franklin wore dresses and sported long blond curls until he was five years old. In accordance with the upper-class fashions of the day, he then abandoned skirts for kilts and Little Lord Fauntleroy suits.

Roosevelt's birthplace in the lush Hudson River valley of New York. Situated on a knoll which commanded a panoramic view, the mansion did not have its present wings at the time of Franklin's birth, 30 January 1882.

James Roosevelt's first wife died in 1876, and four years later, aged 52, he married Sara Delano, who was half his age. Like her husband, Sara Delano came from an extremely prosperous merchant family. James Roosevelt had inherited a comfortable fortune and his greatest concern, especially after his second marriage, was his country squire's life among the Hudson River gentry. As long as his financial investments yielded sufficient money to support this type of luxury, James remained content.

Franklin grew up as an only child with the loving and doting attention of his parents and every privilege of an aristocratic boyhood. Both his parents surrounded young Franklin with luxury that only money and tradition could purchase. There were always many servants at Springwood during Franklin's childhood—a butler, cooks, maids, gardeners and horse groomers. Because of this, after Franklin's birth James and Sara were able to continue their social life, their travels, and their life of affluence.

In later years Sara Delano Roosevelt claimed that neither she or her husband ever tried to influence young Franklin against his own tastes and inclinations or to shape his life. It is hard to imagine, however, a mother more closely attached to a son or more preoccupied with monitoring his life and activities. (James, Franklin's father, died in 1900 at the age of 72. Franklin was then 18.) His strong-willed mother expected that Franklin would, in due course, continue in the Delano and Roosevelt traditions of overseeing the family fortune. "I know that traditionally every mother believes her son will one day be president," Sara Delano Roosevelt remarked in 1932, "but much as I love tradition and believe in perpetuating good ones, that is one to which I never happened to subscribe."

Before he was 15, Franklin had accompanied his parents on eight European trips, each of several months' duration. In Europe his parents socialized with the wealthy aristocracy. With the exception of servants, rarely did young Franklin have contact with people who worked for their living. (When he accompanied his parents on business trips in America, they travelled in a private railway car-

Franklin had a very happy and secure childhood on the Roosevelt estate, where his father taught him to swim, skate, and ride. His playmates were the children of other prominent Hyde Park families, and it was in their company that he grew used to a life of leisure and luxury befitting his social standing.

riage.) Indeed, Franklin's boyhood was the happy boyhood of a young patrician—frequent trips abroad, summers swimming and sailing at the family vacation home on Campobello Island off the coast of Maine, and part of almost each year in New York City. Above all, Hyde Park remained Franklin Roosevelt's true home. Growing up there was indeed idyllic, and Roosevelt, throughout his life, even when he was president, affectionately returned to this magnificent rambling estate. Probably no president had a happier or more secure childhood than did Franklin Roosevelt.

Young Franklin was educated by private tutors and governesses. He seemed fascinated with history and geography. At the age of nine, encouraged by his mother, Franklin started a postage stamp collection, to which he continuously added even when president. He became fluent in French and he

One-year-old Franklin on the shoulder of his father, James. James Roosevelt (1828–1900) was a descendant of Nicholas R. Roosevelt, who emigrated to the New World from Holland during the 1640s.

Young Franklin spent many childhood summers at Campobello, a small island off the coast of Canada. It was at this favourite retreat that James Roosevelt presented his son with a magnificent yacht, the *New Moon*, in 1898.

Franklin at the age of 11 with his mother, Sara Delano Roosevelt (1854–1941). Sara, who said of Franklin that "he was a Delano, not a Roosevelt at all", took a keen interest in her son's upbrining and faced his departure for formal schooling in 1896 with considerable anxiety.

could read and write German. (During World War II, Roosevelt was able to converse with the French general Charles de Gaulle, who refused to speak anything but French.)

Aside from formal subjects, Franklin was tutored in carpentry—making model boats, birdhouses, and toys. He collected birds' eggs and nests, carefully recording his observations in a notebook. When he was 11, he wrote a composition on "Birds of the Hudson River Valley" which so impressed his maternal grandfather that he gave Franklin a life membership in New York's American Museum of Natural History. Photography also fascinated young Franklin. Dozens of family photographs and self-photographs —made possible by the invention of the self-timer— were taken by him using an expensive tripod-mounted Kodak. Many of these photos are now on display in the Roosevelt Museum at Hyde Park.

Throughout his life Roosevelt loved reading. As a teenager, he especially liked books about the sea and naval affairs. Years later, he fondly recalled the boyhood hours spent reading old naval logs and reports found in his maternal grandfather's attic. Undoubtedly, his mother's stirring stories of her seafaring ancestors and of her own travels to Asia as a young woman greatly contributed to this interest.

Springwood had a fine family library, and Franklin, before he had reached 14, had read Alfred T. Mahan's epoch-making *The Influence of Sea Power Upon History*, as well as books written by Mark Twain, Rudyard Kipling, and Francis Parkman. (At the Roosevelt Museum, one can read margin notes and comments made by young Franklin in many of these books.) One afternoon, his mother found him engrossed in reading *Webster's Unabridged Dictionary*. She asked "what on earth" he was doing. He replied that he was reading the dictionary because "there are lots words I don't understand" and that he was "almost half way through".

In the autumn of 1986 Sara and James Roosevelt registered Franklin at the Groton School in Massachussetts. Their aim was to prepare Franklin for college. This was the first time that Franklin would be attending a formal school, and also the first time that he would be separated from his loving parents.

Young Franklin roams the Hyde Park woods armed with a bow and arrows. It was in such beautiful surroundings that he first began to take a keen interest in the study of wildlife.

Franklin astride his pony, Debby. To provide his son with a sense of responsibility, James Roosevelt always asked that Franklin take care of his own pets.

As a student at Groton Roosevelt often feared that he would not pass examinations. During his first year he received mainly Cs but later brought his average grade up to B.

Despite his enjoyment of sports, the young Roosevelt was never much of an athlete. In fact, his principal contribution to the Groton School's sports programme was to manage the school's baseball team.

Mrs Roosevelt recorded Franklin's departure in her diary: "We dusted his birds and he had a swim in the river . . .I looked on. And with heavy heart. It is hard to leave our darling boy. James and I both feel this parting very much."

Groton was an upmarket prep school for rich boys from old, respectable families whose children were on their way to one of the Ivy League universities. Franklin spent four years at Groton, four years which made a lasting impact upon him. Throughout his life he maintained a friendship with Groton's rector and headmaster, Endicott Peabody. When Franklin married, Peabody performed the ceremony, and when Franklin took his first presidential inaugural oath in 1933, Peabody recited the prayer.

At Groton, Franklin's grades averaged slightly less than B. There were 19 in his class—all boys from similar upper-class backgrounds. "Very good," remarked headmaster Peabody on Franklin's first monthly report to his parents. "He strikes me as an intelligent and faithful scholar, and a good boy."

Compared with the comforts of Springwood, Groton was almost spartan. Franklin's tiny room was sparsely furnished. A curtain hung in place of a door. The boys were awakened at 7 a.m.; breakfast was at 7.30; morning chapel at 8.15; and then off to classes. Lunch was served at noon followed by more classes and compulsory athletics. At supper the boys wore starched white collars and black patent-leather shoes. Then followed evening chapel and study hour.

The curriculum at Groton stressed the classics. In his first year, for example, Franklin studied Latin, Greek, algebra, English literature and composition, ancient history, science, and Bible studies. Franklin ranked in the top quarter of students throughout his four years at Groton. Never a great student, never overly popular with his fellow classmates, he did enjoy the distinction one year of being Groton's champion "high kicker" in football. In his final report to Franklin's mother, headmaster Peabody wrote: "He has been a thoroughly faithful scholar and a most satisfactory member of this school. I part with Franklin with reluctance."

He was a quiet, satisfactory boy, of more than ordinary intelligence, taking a good position in his form, but not brilliant. Athletically he was rather too slight for success. We all liked him.
–ENDICOTT PEABODY
rector of Groton School

Roosevelt much admired and loved Endicott Peabody, the rector and headmaster of Groton School.

2

Student Years

The Harvard University of 1900 that Franklin Roosevelt entered as a freshman seemed very removed from the problems of the United States. The country had been rapidly transformed from a predominantly rural, agrarian society into a highly industrialized one. The country had become a modern nation, a world power. The continent had been conquered, the frontier virtually ended. Population had grown from 30 million in 1860 to 75 million in 1900, mostly due to the hordes of immigrants who flocked to America seeking a better life. But the promise of that life and the wonders of modern technology also brought crowded cities and great inequality in the distribution of wealth.

At the beginning of the 20th century there were hundreds of new inventions which were changing the lives of most people—motion pictures, lifts, underground railways, telephones, and cars, to name but a few. Because of corporate consolidations, one per cent of American corporations controlled more than a third of American manufacturing. One reason for the great growth of industry was the cheap labour supply (one per cent of the families in America controlled about 90 per cent of the nation's wealth). Workers in the mills and factories were painfully aware of how low their standard of living remained in comparison with that of their employers. The average daily wage for a worker was but US $1.50 per day.

In 1907 Franklin and Eleanor moved into a fashionable New York City townhouse (left) constructed for them by Sara Roosevelt.

Roosevelt entered Harvard in September 1900 with many of his former Groton classmates. Fortunately for the future president, admission to the university at the turn of the century depended more on family background than academic ability and attainments.

Like cousin Theodore before him, Franklin ventured to New York City soon after his Harvard graduation. There, on the city's streets the young aristocrat saw how the less privileged lived.

Women and children worked in factories for wages as low as $6 a week. Child labour had become a national disgrace. At least 1.7 million children under 16 worked in factories and in the fields; 10 per cent of all girls between 10 and 15 and 20 per cent of all boys worked. In New York City two-thirds of the residents lived in dirty and crowded tenements. Inadequate housing, poor sanitation, and low wages were but a few of the problems faced by millions of Americans in 1900.

Harvard University in 1900 was, as it had been for some 250 years, a school for the sons of America's most distinguished and wealthy families. Almost immediately, Franklin Roosevelt, now 18, plunged into a wide range of social, athletic, and extracurricular activities. He seemed released from the confines of Springwood and Groton. He tried out for nearly every athletic team but got into only one intramural football team. Although he was now over six feet (two metres) tall, he weighed only 145 pounds (65 kilograms), which was much too light for the varsity team. He was too slow for the athletic team and not strong enough to succeed at rowing. Though he joined the freshman choral society, in his second year he lost out to better voices. His main interest became Harvard's undergraduate daily newspaper, *The Harvard Crimson*. During his junior year he was elected editor-in-chief.

Young Roosevelt read history and government, with English and public speaking as subsidiary courses. Roosevelt was not a great student. In fact, he did not seem to take his studies that seriously. As a result, his grades were usually a "gentleman's C". Charming, handsome, extremely wealthy, Franklin was also a distant cousin of Theodore Roosevelt, who, upon the death of William McKinley in 1901, became president of the United States.

During Franklin's freshman year, his father died. James, who was 72, had bequeathed to his son an

New York's Lower East Side in the 1900s was a magnet for the poor and newly arrived immigrants flooding into the country. It also gave Roosevelt his first real glimpse of widespread poverty and suffering.

**Harvard's club system at the
turn of the century was
extremely elitist. Franklin
did manage to get into the
"Hasty Pudding" but was
bitter about being passed by
"Porcellian", the even more
exclusive club that years
earlier had admitted his
cousin, Theodore Roose-
velt.**

annual income of about $6,000. (A male school-
teacher in 1900 earned about $500 a year so $6,000
was indeed a fortune.) His mother received Springwood and the rest of the estate. (In addition, Sara
had inherited more than $1 million when her father
died in 1898.) In his will James had stipulated that
he wanted Franklin "under the supervision of his
mother" and shortly after her husband's death Sara
Roosevelt, now 46, rented an apartment a short
distance from Harvard to be near her son.

The presence of Franklin's mother so close to
Harvard gained him a quite unjustified reputation
as a "mama's boy". And, while many a young lady
was put off by his domineering mother's influence
on him, Franklin had learned how to handle her.
Sometimes he gave parties in his mother's lavishly
furnished apartment, but at other times he
remained independent of her presence. He was not
a snob. He worked with poor children and he raised
money for a variety of charities. Yet he remained a
Roosevelt who was invited to White House social

By 1900, Harvard had long been a citadel of learning for the sons of America's most prestigious, wealthiest families. With his good looks, outgoing personality, and upper-class connections, Roosevelt felt quite at home. He did not, however, distinguish himself as a scholar, graduating with a C average.

Although Franklin and Eleanor (1884–1962) had known one another almost from infancy, their romance did not blossom until Roosevelt's Harvard days. Sara, Franklin's mother, disapproved of the shy and awkward Eleanor and tried, without success, to break up the romance.

functions. It was social activities rather than scholarship that occupied most of his time at Harvard.

The most important event of his years at Harvard was his engagement to his fifth cousin, Anna Eleanor Roosevelt. Franklin had known Eleanor since she was a child, but their relationship did not blossom into romance until his final year in 1903. Their engagement was announced in November 1904 and their marriage took place in New York City on 17 March 1905. Franklin was 23 and Eleanor 21. President Theodore Roosevelt, Eleanor's uncle, gave the bride away. The president was the main attraction at the wedding while the bride and groom were virtually ignored.

While there had long been ties of affection between Eleanor and Franklin, there were also major differences of personality and background that made the match seem a most unlikely prospect. While Franklin's secure and protected boyhood had given him enormous self-confidence, Eleanor's childhood had been less fortunate. Her father, Theodore Roosevelt's brother, had been an alcoholic and her mother had been extremely cruel to her. Because her mother died when she was eight and her father died when she was ten, Eleanor was raised in the very strict and unloving home of her grandmother. When she was 15, for example, she went to a teenage party at a relative's house. Her grandmother had made her wear a dress suitable for a little girl and she felt terribly ashamed of it. She was having a miserable time until the best looking boy at the party, Franklin Roosevelt, asked her to dance. He may have done so simply because he saw that she was alone and having a dull time. But from that moment on, Franklin became someone very special to Eleanor. And, several years later, when Franklin courted her, Eleanor seemed frightened. His proposal of marriage made her very happy but, as she explained in her autobiography, she wasn't sure why this desirable young man chose her to wed.

Eleanor had come to womanhood feeling most unsure of herself. (She recalled the many painful times when her mother called her "Granny" as a

As editor of *The Harvard Crimson*, FDR gave no indication of deep political concern or ambition. In fact, his most indignant editorials tended to address such banal issues as weak cheering at football games, fire protection for the dormitories, and the need for new campus sidewalks.

child. Often her mother would explain to visitors: "She is such a funny child, so old-fashioned, that we always call her 'Granny'." Eleanor at such times "would sink through the floor in shame".) While Franklin was handsome, charming, and enormously popular, she was plain, not very rich, and not very pretty. While he was athletic and gregarious, she was serious and withdrawn beyond her years. Nevertheless, their relationship thrived.

At first, Franklin did not tell his mother about his growing interest in Eleanor. When he finally announced his intention of marrying his cousin, Sara Roosevelt was shocked. She was not pleased at the thought of another woman in her son's life. She tried to cool the relationship by urging the couple to wait before formally committing themselves. In an attempt to have Franklin forget Eleanor, she took him on a Caribbean cruise. And upon hearing of a minor diplomatic post available in London, Sara attempted to use her connections to secure the position for Franklin so he would be forced to leave the country. In the end her efforts failed. With grace and charm she finally welcomed Eleanor into the family.

From this point on, to understand Franklin's life, we must understand Eleanor *and* Franklin, for they complemented each other in so many ways. Each became a great national figure and each exerted a strong influence over the other. Eleanor's concern for the needy and her extremely sensitive nature were strong factors in shaping Franklin's social outlook.

Franklin and Eleanor delayed their honeymoon so that he could finish his first year at Columbia University Law School. Then, in June 1905, they took a grand European trip. Their family connections with Theodore Roosevelt earned them lavish treatment wherever they went. Upon their return to New York City, the young couple lived in a small house at 125 East 36th Street which had been rented and furnished for them by Franklin's mother. "For the first year of my married life," Eleanor later recalled, "my mother-in-law did everything for me."

> *I do so want you to learn to love me a little. You must know that I will always try to do what you wish, for I have grown to love you very dearly during the past summer.*
> —ELEANOR ROOSEVELT
> to Franklin Roosevelt, in 1903

Roosevelt's mother thought Franklin too young to marry and thus took him on a Caribbean cruise to thwart the romance. But Franklin and Eleanor were married on 17 March 1905, and her uncle, Theodore Roosevelt (1858–1919)—inaugurated president only two weeks before—came from the White House to give the bride away.

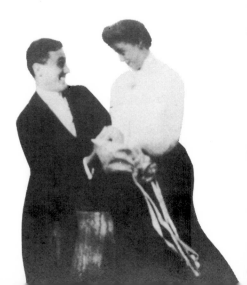

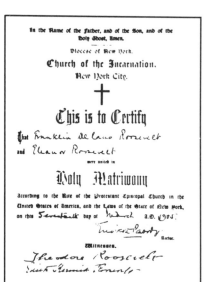

President Theordore Roosevelt and his First Lady were the witnesses at the wedding of Franklin and Eleanor. The Reverend Mr Peabody, Franklin's old headmaster at Groton, officiated. The newlyweds went on a grand tour of Europe for their honeymoon.

The newly married Franklin and Eleanor Roosevelt. At the wedding the boisterous President Roosevelt stole the show. "When he goes to a wedding, he wants to be the bride and when he goes to a funeral, he wants to be the corpse", one guest remarked sourly.

In the spring of 1907 Franklin passed the New York State Bar examination and decided not to finish his degree at Columbia. Now 25, he seemed perfectly suited to lead the life of a country squire, just as his father had. The young couple had an annual income from trust funds of more than $12,000. (An average factory worker at that time earned about $300 per year.) Their first child, Anna Eleanor, was born on 3 May 3 1906. Anna was followed by James in 1907; the first Franklin Jr, who died shortly after birth in 1909; Elliott in 1910; the second Franklin Jr in 1914; and John in 1916. As Eleanor noted, for the first 12 years of her marriage, she was "always getting over a baby or having one".

Franklin and Eleanor with their first child, Anna
Eleanor, born in 1906. They had four sons: James,
Elliott, Franklin Jr, and John.

3

The Making of a Politician

In 1910, much to the surprise of his family and friends, Franklin Roosevelt entered the world of politics. Although a great admirer of his distant cousin Theodore Roosevelt, a progressive Republican, Franklin, like his father, was a registered Democrat. Nominated by New York Democrats for state senator from the 26th District (Columbia, Dutchess, and Putnam counties), Roosevelt eagerly plunged into the race. (Though no Democrat had been elected from this district since 1856!) He rented a bright red Maxwell touring car—perhaps the first time a car had been used in a local political race—and spent a month strenuously visiting every part of the sprawling district. Often accompanied by Eleanor, he made an average of ten speeches a day, usually in the small farming communities that dotted the eastern side of the Hudson River valley.

Franklin thrived on speaking with farmers, workers and whoever would listen to him. Not all of the Democratic leadership was pleased with the selection of Franklin. Some criticized his rich background and his Harvard accent. Regardless, they assumed that whoever the Democrats would have nominated would be defeated. Roosevelt seemed personable, and greeted people with the salutation

In 1910 Roosevelt entered politics, standing as a Democratic candidate (Theodore Roosevelt, his cousin, was a Republican) for the New York State Senate. He beat the incumbent by 1,140 votes. Said Democratic Party boss Timothy Sullivan: "This fellow is still young. Wouldn't it be safer to drown him before he grows up?"

Josephus Daniels (1862–1948), the influential southern newspaper publisher who became Woodrow Wilson's secretary of the navy.

The first published caricature of FDR appeared in the *New York Herald* in 1911.

A political flier used by Roosevelt in his 1912 campaign for reelection to the New York State Senate.

"My Friends", which soon became his political trademark. His personal warmth, especially in one-to-one talks with his neighbours, paved the way for an unexpected victory. Much to the surprise of even the Democratic leadership, Franklin won the election, receiving 15,708 votes to 14,568 votes for his opponent—an unprecendented result for a Domocratic candidate in this area.

When Roosevelt took his seat in Albany, New York, in 1911, the state legislature still chose the state's United States senators. (This was changed by the 17th Amendment to the Constitution in 1913.) While the Democrats held a majority in the legislature, Roosevelt became the head of a group which effectively blocked the senatorial selection of the Democratic political bosses. This political independence on his part gave the freshman legislator a great deal of publicity. "Take my advice," one seasoned Republican legislator advised a Democratic colleague, "and drown him before he grows old and tough."

During his two years in Albany, Roosevelt became committed to conservation. He also began to grasp workers' concerns. This won him the support of the New York State Labour Federation in his 1912 campaign for reelection. Roosevelt won easily. But due to an attack to typhoid fever, he had left his campaign to Louis Howe, a journalist whom he befriended in Albany. Until his death in 1936, Howe remained Franklin's closest political adviser.

In 1912 Woodrow Wilson, a Democrat, was elected president of the United States—the second Democrat to achieve this high office since the end of the Civil War. Roosevelt had been an early supporter of Wilson and, on 4 March 1913, he and Eleanor attended Wilson's inauguration in Washington. On the morning of the swearing in, Roosevelt met Josephus Daniels, whom Wilson had appointed secretary of the navy.

"How would you like to come to Washington as assistant secretary of the navy?" asked Daniels.

"I would like it bully well," responded Franklin, his face beaming with pleasure. President Wilson approved and the appointment was officially made.

On 17 March 1913, the eighth anniversary of his marriage to Eleanor, Franklin Roosevelt, now 31, found himself in the navy department sitting at cousin Theodore Roosevelt's old desk. (Theodore Roosevelt had been assistant secretary of the navy from 1897 to 1898.) "It is interesting," the former president wrote to Franklin, "that you are in another place which I myself once had." (Theodore had also started his career in the New York state legislature and served from 1883 to 1885.) Franklin Roosvelt had now been in politics for less than three years.

Franklin Roosevelt's seven years as assistant secretary of the navy (1913–20) proved an excellent training for his later service as a wartime president. He inspected ships and naval stations. "I get my fingers into everything," he boasted. When a navy submarine sank with all its crew members, he immediately went out in another to demonstrate his confidence in the underwater craft. He assisted

You know the Roosevelts, don't you? Whenever a Roosevelt rides, he wishes to ride in front.
—ELIHU ROOT
speaking in 1913

Roosevelt at his desk in the New York State Senate chamber in Albany. Elected as a Democrat in a normally Republican district, he served as a state senator from 1910 to 1913, when he resigned to become assistant secretary of the navy in Washington, D.C.

<blockquote>
I get my fingers into everything, and there's no law against it.

—FRANKLIN ROOSEVELT
speaking in 1913, when he was
assistant secretary of the navy
</blockquote>

Assistant Secretary of the Navy Roosevelt practises marksmanship with a Springfield rifle at the United States Marine Corps range at Winthrop, Maryland, in 1916.

President Woodrow Wilson (1856–1924) returns from the Versailles peace conference in 1919. Wilson failed to gain public support or Senate approval of the treaty that brought World War I to an end.

in programmes to modernize the navy and to reduce red tape.

Eleanor joined Franklin in Washington and, again, because of their social prominence and their relationship to Theodore Roosevelt, the couple was warmly welcomed by Washington society. (Theodore Roosevelt died in 1919.) Franklin was an ideal conversationalist—always charming, always the attentive listener. He seems to have had an enormous amount of energy—a man "breathing health and virility", in the words of a military aide at the British embassy. His family life seemed ideal. James, Franklin's oldest son, described his father as "the handsomest, strongest, most glamorous, vigorous, physical father in the world". His children adored him—Franklin was always there for family picnics, outings, and celebrations. Sometimes he took the children to the navy department where James and Elliott were fascinated by the model ships which lined the corridors. "There is only one thing that interferes with their perfect enjoyment," Roosevelt noted, "and that is my inability to take the boats out of the 'windows,' as they call the glass cases, and sail them in the bathtub."

In 1914 war broke out in Europe and by 1917 what everyone dreaded, happened—the United States became involved. The responsibilities of the assistant secretary of the navy increased. Franklin supervised programmes to bolster U.S. naval strength. He became engaged in naval strategy sessions. He made many inspection trips to industrial plants to oversee efficiency. The navy was expanding—more ships, more men, and more up-to-date arms. And Franklin Roosevelt was involved in the decision-making process.

This experience of a nation at war enormously influenced him and he rapidly learned about government management in a time of crisis—of how things happen on a colossal scale. In July 1918 Roosevelt toured the European battlefields to inspect military installations. (In later years, Roosevelt considered this trip to France in the midst of the war as one of the great adventures of his life.) And when the war ended in November 1918 Roosevelt became active in the many problems of naval demobilization.

America's involvement in World War I changed the United States. The country was now actively caught up in Europe's affairs. President Wilson attended

The German sinking of the British superline *Lusitania* **on 7 May 1915, with the loss of 1,198 lives—128 of them American—hastened the U.S. entry into World War I. Germany published an advance warning in American newspapers. Here the ship is seen leaving New York on its last, ill-fated voyage.**

Long before women were recruited for the Women's Auxiliary Corps, Washington used feminine wiles to build up its military ranks, as shown in this World War I poster by Howard Chandler Christie.

GEE !!
I WISH I WERE
A MAN
I'd JOIN
The NAVY

BE A MAN AND DO IT
UNITED STATES NAVY
RECRUITING STATION

This is not a question of war or peace. I take it that there are as many advocates of arbitration and international peace in the navy as in any other profession. But we are confronted with a condition—the fact that our nation has decided in the past to have a fleet, and that war is still a possibility.

—FRANKLIN ROOSEVELT
speaking to members of the Navy
League of the United States in 1913

the peace conference at Versailles in France in 1919, and he agreed that the United States would join the newly created League of Nations. At home, however, many Americans believed that the United States should not get entangled in Europe's affairs. Roosevelt, having seen first-hand the destruction caused by the war, supported American membership in the League of Nations as a practical way to prevent future wars. He admitted that the idea was experimental but the "general plan" was sound. "I have read the draft of the League three times," he wrote, "and always find something to object to in it, and that is the way with everybody...Personally, I am willing to make a try." Not to join the League, he thought, would do "grievous wrong" to America "and to all mankind". As a world power, the United States now had to participate in world affairs. Roosevelt had no prominent part in the fight for Senate approval of American membership in the League of Nations, but he witnessed it all, and he remembered what he saw. In the end the Senate did not ratify the Versailles Treaty and the United States did not join the League of Nations.

In July 1920 Franklin Roosevelt was a delegate to the Democratic National Convention in San Francisco. The defeat of the motion proposing American membership in the League of Nations by the Senate, and President Wilson's illness, which had greatly limited his ability, confused and divided the Democratic Party as it met to nominate its candidates for president and vice-president. The Democrats nominated Governor James Cox of Ohio for president and, much to Franklin's surprise, the convention chose him, at the age of 38, as their candidate for vice-president. (Governor Cox later wrote that although he did not know Roosevelt, he preferred him as a running mate because Roosevelt came from New York and balanced the ticket geographically.)

The team of Cox and Roosevelt campaigned in support of Wilson's ideals. Roosevelt proved himself an attractive national candidate and a tireless campaigner. While vice-presidential nominees usually remained on the sidelines, the energetic Roosevelt dashed around the country. His speeches

The draft—today's Selective Service System—became a hard fact of life, at least for able-bodied men, in World War I. Here Secretary of War Newton D. Baker (1871–1937), blindfolded, draws the first draftee's number.

At the age of 38 FDR was nominated for vice-president of the United States, with James M. Cox (1870–1957) running for president on the Democratic ticket in 1920. They lost to Republicans Warren G. Harding (1865–1923) and Calvin Coolidge (1872–1933). Here, Roosevelt accepts the Democratic vice-presidential nomination at Hyde Park, N.Y. before a crowd of his neighbours and friends in 1920.

Roosevelt took the Democrats' 1920 defeat graciously and philosophically. "The moment of defeat," he told a friend, "is the best time to lay plans for future victories."

were impressive. He had a superb command of the English language and he varied his words to suit each particular audience. He spoke about conservation, education, the abuses of child labour, and of the need for a League of Nations.

Roosevelt fully expected that the Republicans would win the election because the League of Nations issue had so deeply divided the Democrats. And the Republican team of Warren Hardin and Calvin Coolidge did win, carrying 37 states and compiling an electoral triumph of 404–127. Although the defeat did not surprise Roosevelt, the magnitude of it did. Indeed, Harding and Coolidge received almost twice as many popular votes as did

Cox and Roosevelt. Not since James Monroe's defeat of John Quincy Adams in 1820, exactly a century before, had a presidential election been so lopsided. The Republicans owed their triumph to the failure of the Democrats to achieve the better nation and the better world which President Wilson had so often described as his objective.

Harding's talk of a return to "normalcy" seemed more attractive. The team of Cox and Roosevelt could not persuade the nation otherwise. Yet, Franklin Roosevelt regarded the experience as a valuable episode in his political apprenticeship. "Curiously enough," he wrote to a friend three days after the election, "I do not feel in the least bit down-hearted."

Young Roosevelt is very promising, but I should think he'd wear himself out in the promiscuous and extended contacts he maintains with people. But as I have observed him, he seems to clarify his ideas and teach himself as he goes along by that very conversational method.
—NEWTON D. BAKER
U.S. secretary of war from 1916 to 1921

James M. Cox (left), the 1920 Democratic presidential candidate, chose Roosevelt as his running mate because of the latter's service in the Wilson administration, his record as a moderate "dry" (Prohibition was the law in 1920), and his reputation for political independence.

4

Crisis Years

Disaster struck in August 1921. While vacationing at his summer home at Campobello, Roosevelt was stricken with polio. He was 39 years old, the father of five young children. At first, the local doctors thought he had the flu—then called grippe. But Roosevelt grew worse and suffered dreadful pain. A specialist called from Boston discovered that it was far worse than the flu—it was infantile paralysis, or polio. (The Salk vaccine against polio was not developed until 1955.) Roosevelt was then taken to a New York City hospital. "I cannot say how long Mr Roosevelt will be kept in the hospital," his doctor told reporters, "but you can say definitely that he will not be crippled."

Roosevelt believed hopefully in his doctor's diagnosis. But the true situation soon became evident. "He has such courage, such ambition," the doctor wrote, "yet at the same time such an extraordinarily sensitive emotional mechanism that it will take all the skill which he can muster to lead him successfully to a recognition of what he really faces without crushing him."

The disease had left Roosevelt's legs paralyzed. He would never walk again. His mother wanted him to retire to the quiet life of a country gentleman at Hyde Park, overseeing his financial investments and indulging in his many hobbies. But his wife, Eleanor, and Louis Howe, his devoted friend, felt otherwise. With their help Franklin maintained his ties with politics. The two brought him political

Despite his unflagging optimism that he would one day be cured, Roosevelt was forced to wear heavy steel braces for the rest of his life. He is shown here with John W. Davis (1873–1955), who won the 1924 Democratic nomination over Alfred E. Smith (1873–1944), whom Roosevelt had nominated.

Crippled by polio at the age of 39, Roosevelt found the waters at Warm Springs, Georgia, helpful, and he developed the resort into a famous hydrotherapeutic center. Here he turns on the valve of a newly constructed water system at a dedication ceremony.

news. They wrote hundreds of letters for him to political leaders all over the country.

Above all, Eleanor and Louis Howe reminded him that his brain had not been affected, only his legs. They put spirit into Franklin when he needed it the most. As the physical pain eased, they brought dozens of visitors to see him, especially people from the world of politics. They encouraged arguments and discussions about bringing the Democratic Party back from its 1920 defeat.

Roosevelt resolved never to appear helpless, dependent, or defeated by his affliction. Whether in public or in private, he never failed to smile. In short, the disease revealed that Franklin had a supply of sheer determination so large that even those closest to him were surprised and admiring. He learned to use his upper body's strength to hoist himself from a special light wheelchair into any chair he wanted to use for work or talk. (Roosevelt devised this wheelchair, now on display at the Roosevelt Museum at Hyde Park, from a cut-down kitchen chair.)

He had a small car rebuilt in such a way that he could drive it without using foot pedals. He learned to stand erect, leaning on a table or on a lecture stand, but he always needed his heavy steel braces, which weighed seven pounds each, to keep his legs from buckling. Through this physical ordeal, Roosevelt managed to keep a smiling face. He minimized every setback while maximizing every improvement. He bore it all, remembered Eleanor, "without the slightest complaint." James Roosevelt, Franklin's son, wrote that "it was not polio that forged Father's character but that it was Father's character that enabled him to rise above the affliction."

In 1924 Roosevelt heard that the warm mineral waters of a Southern health spa could help polio victims. On his first visit to Warm Springs, Georgia, he found that as soon as he lowered himself into the mineral water, a "heavenly warmth" flowed over his legs. "How marvellous it feels," he said, "I don't think I'll ever get out." Because of the 88-degree temperature of the water and its buoyancy, Roosevelt could remain in the pool for hours—swimming,

Louis McHenry Howe (1870–1936), Albany correspondent for a New York paper, was called in as Roosevelt's political advisor in 1912 and remained with him for the rest of his life. A dour man, disliked by Eleanor, Howe was Roosevelt's political mentor, coaching him in the intricate thrusts and parries of American politics.

floating, and kicking his legs. While no miracle occurred at Warm Springs, Roosevelt certainly benefited from the warm water, the sun, and the relaxed atmosphere. In fact, it was here in Warm Springs, more than anywhere else, that Roosevelt found help for his condition.

He purchased the resort in 1926, and established close ties with this small rural community, making regular visits there throughout his life. He spent about $200,000, almost two-thirds of his private wealth, into rehabilitating the spa and making it permanently available for his own use and for others in similar need. He transformed Warm Springs into a centre for the treatment of polio victims.

Franklin Roosevelt's illness obviously had a profound impact on his life. This athletic, dynamic man who had enormous drive and energy, now at the age of 39, was a cripple, completely dependent on others for his basic needs. Eleanor, perhaps for this reason, believed that the polio ordeal made

Frank Roosevelt is physically as good as he ever was in his life. His whole trouble is his lack of muscular control of his lower limbs. But a governor does not have to be an acrobat. We do not elect him for his ability to do a double back-flip or a handspring. The work of the governorship is brainwork.
—AL SMITH
speaking in 1928

Roosevelt swimming in the pool at Warm Springs, where warm water heavy with mineral salts enabled polio patients to exercise without overtiring. Roosevelt went to Warm Springs regularly, and it was there that he died in April 1945.

Roosevelt liked the simplicity of Warm Springs, where the spa was little more than a run-down inn before he took it over. This is a photograph of the village's main street, taken when Franklin Roosevelt visited there in 1933 for the first Thanksgiving Day of his presidency.

Franklin more compassionate towards the problems of the common people. Roosevelt rarely spoke of his affliction, although he once told a friend of how he had spent two years trying desperately to wiggle his big toe and how he finally succeeded. After that, he said, he would never believe that anything is impossible.

Almost everyone who knew Franklin wrote their recollections of his illness. In fact, almost everyone who knew Franklin Roosevelt has written about him! The Roosevelts, especially his mother, kept virtually every item associated with his life. Rarely was anything thrown away. Franklin and his family were letter writers. Wherever they were, whatever they did, they carefully described in detailed letters to family members and to friends. Many kept diaries, including Roosevelt's mother and his wife, and much of this material has been preserved.

We even have fairly detailed accounts of Franklin's extramarital affair with Lucy Mercer—an affair which almost led to a break up of his marriage while he was assistant secretary of the navy. Eleanor thought this affair had ended in 1920. It now seems that it continued throughout his life. In fact, Lucy Mercer was with Franklin in Warm Springs on the day he died.

Of all the presidents of the United States, Franklin Roosevelt's life is undoubtedly the most carefully documented. We can see his life, his illness, we can see Roosevelt through the eyes of many—the missing link is Franklin Roosevelt himself. He never wrote a memoir, nor an autobiography, nor did he keep a personal diary. Therefore, we do not know *his* inner feelings, *his* personal thoughts. In other words, we do not know what made Franklin tick, except through the memories and words of others.

At the Roosevelt Museum in Hyde Park we can visit his beautiful home and share the views of the Hudson River valley that he loved so much. We can see his childhood toys, his stuffed birds, the books he read, the clothing he wore, even his braces which were strapped around his legs. But, despite this vast documentation, he still remains elusive, a

The young man who had strode down convention aisles looking like a Greek god now had to be carried around like a baby, or pushed in a wheelchair. The man of only 40 who had struck everyone with his animation and vitality spent hours crawling on the floor as he tried to learn to walk again.
—JAMES MACGREGOR BURNS
from *Roosevelt: The Lion and the Fox*

Dr Jonas Salk, (left), developer of the polio vaccine, and Basil O'Connor, Roosevelt's former law partner, are shown here with Mrs Roosevelt at the dedication of the Polio Hall of Fame in Warm Springs, Georgia, in 1959.

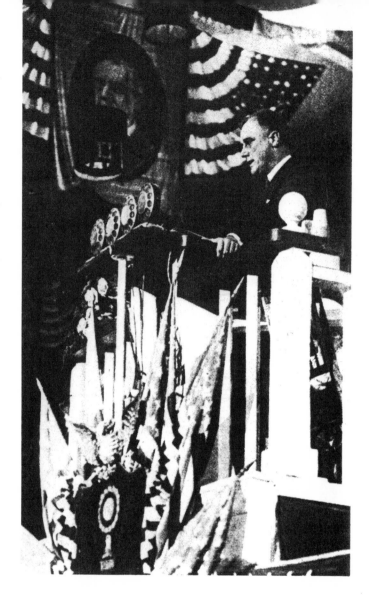

At the 1924 Domocratic convention, Roosevelt nominated Governor Alfred E. Smith of New York for the presidency, dubbing him "the Happy Warrior", a label that Smith then carried for the rest of his life.

bit of a mystery. The inner, the personal dynamics of this complicated man are still missing. Hence, we cannot answer several important questions about his life, especially in regard to his close relationship with his mother, whom he loved dearly, and with his wife, whom he equally loved. We cannot explain, from Franklin's point of view, the influence of his distant cousin, Theodore Roosevelt. Was Theodore his idol? Did he model his professional career using the former president as his example? Did he marry Eleanor because she was Theodore Roosevelt's niece?

During his illness the people closest to Franklin pulled him in different directions. His mother demanded that he retire to Hyde Park, while his wife and Louis Howe pushed him to conquer his physical handicap and to resume his promising political career. For Eleanor, the first years of Franklin's illness were the most difficult of her life. She had to raise five children, deal with a very sick husband, and handle her domineering mother-in-law. For the first time in her marriage, Eleanor defied her mother-in-law's wishes. Franklin would not retire! Eleanor, at last, had become independent of Sara—and at the 1924 Democratic National Convention, Franklin Roosevelt made his choice. He returned to politics and to a great personal victory.

The high point of the 1924 Democratic convention was Franklin's speech nominating New York Governor Alfred E. Smith to be the Democratic Party's candidate for president. (A divided Democratic convention eventually chose John W. Davis, former ambassador to Great Britain, on the 103rd ballot.) Franklin did not want to be seen in a wheelchair and so with the help of his son James,

An early photograph of Lucy Mercer Rutherford, widely known as the "other woman" in FDR's life. In fact it was she, and not Eleanor, who was with Roosevelt at his death.

When President Calvin Coolidge (left) did not "choose to run" for reelection in 1928, Herbert C. Hoover (1874—1964) (right), an Iowa engineer who was well known for his refugee relief efforts during World War I, succeeded him and ran smack into the Great Depression, the dire consequences of which paved the way for Roosevelt's election to the White House.

49

In extremely diverse ways Al Capone, Charles Lindbergh, and Babe Ruth came to symbolize the wild, seemingly carefree pre-Depression period now known as the Roaring Twenties. While Ruth was hitting mammoth home runs, and Lindbergh was thrilling the world with his flying skills, Capone was ruthlessly gunning down rival mobsters in Chicago.

he slowly made his way from the convention floor to the platform to deliver his speech.

"As we walked—struggled, really—down the aisle to the rear of the platform, he leaned heavily on my arm, gripping me so hard it hurt," James wrote. "It was hot, but the heat in that building did not alone account for the perspiration which beaded on his

brow. His hands were wet. His breathing was laboured. Leaning on me with one arm, working a crutch with the other, his legs locked stiffly in his braces, he went on his awkward way." Thunderous cheers swept through the convention hall when Franklin, on crutches, appeared on the speaker's platform. He relaxed his grip on his son's arm. Defying the pain of his braced legs, he slowly, ever so slowly, moved one crutch a few inches ahead of the other. The delegates held their breath, fearing that this gallant man might fall. When he reached the rostrum, he cast aside his crutches, drew himself erect by grasping the lectern, and smiled triumphantly into the spotlight's glare.

Indeed, this was a moment of dramatic heroism. The crowd went wild. The ovation marked a personal triumph. Then, in measured tones, skilfully pacing himself, Roosevelt dominated the audience with his nominating speech for Smith. At the end, the cheering lasted for one hour and 13 minutes. Indeed, this was a rare display of courage and eloquence.

These unhappy times call for the building of plans that rest upon the forgotten, the unorganized but the indispensable units of economic power, for plans... that build from the bottom up and not from the top down, that put their faith once more in the forgotten man at the bottom of the economic pyramid.
—FRANKLIN ROOSEVELT
speaking in 1932

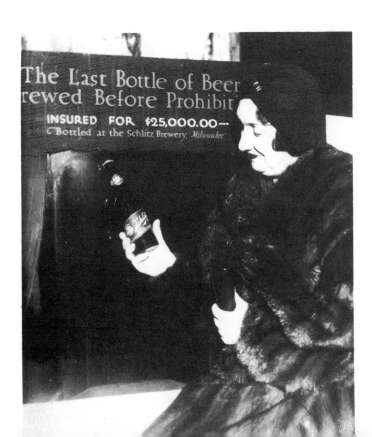

A widely publicized photograph just before Prohibition went into effect in 1920.

5

Apprenticeship in Albany

Roosevelt spent most of the 1920s struggling to walk again. He tried all types of "quack" remedies as well as the most modern medical treatments. But it was at Warm Springs that he found his greatest relief. Early in 1927 he decided to concentrate on rehabilitating other polio victims by forming the nonprofit Georgia Warm Springs Foundation. He began supervising the building of new cottages, he had more pools dug, and he planned new access roads. Within a few years, because of Roosevelt's increasing prominence, Warm Springs became an international centre for the study and treatment of infantile paralysis.

To those who came to Warm Springs for help, he was always "Dr Roosevelt," as his fellow polio-stricken friends called him. "I undertook to be doctor and physiotherapist, all rolled into one . . . I taught them all at least to play around in the water." And, along with the growing professional staff, he worked out charts for measuring muscle growth and developed special water exercises. "You've got to know you're going to improve," he would say. "Keep yourselves mentally alert; don't lose contact with the things you enjoyed before infantile paralysis."

In 1928 the Democratic Party chose Alfred E. Smith as their presidential candidate. Smith was

> *To guard the toilers in the factories and to insure them a fair wage and protection from the dangers of their trades; to open the doors of knowledge to their children more widely; to aid those who are crippled and ill... these great aims of life are more fully realized [in New York] than in any other State in the Union. We have but started on the road, and we have far to go.*
> –FRANKLIN ROOSEVELT speaking at his inauguration as governor of New York, 1 January 1929

After nominating Al Smith for the 1928 presidential campaign, FDR reluctantly agreed to run for governor of New York. Smith lost the nomination but Roosevelt narrowly won the governorship. Here he is at his desk at his New York City campaign headquarters.

Roosevelt greatly enjoyed swimming, which brought a measure of relief to his crippling paralysis. He developed strong shoulders and a powerful backstroke. He would give friends a head start and then, turning on his back with his legs dragging, quickly overtake them with a few tremendous strokes.

Roosevelt with his then close political ally Al Smith, at Hyde Park in 1924. Between them is John W. Davis, who became the Democratic presidential nominee over Smith that year when a deadlock developed at the party's convention. In later years the Roosevelt-Smith friendship cooled considerably.

the first Roman Catholic nominated for president by a major political party. And Franklin once again spoke on behalf of the New York governor, who won on the first ballot. Franklin returned to Warm Springs confident that he had done his part and could spend the rest of the year trying to regain strength in his legs. Franklin also wanted to raise money for his new foundation.

But Smith's campaign started badly. When the New York State Democratic convention met in October, politicians began to doubt if Smith would carry his own state. Without New York, Smith would not have a chance of winning the election. While party strategists thought that Smith would win in New York City, they were doubtful if he could carry upstate New York. Therefore, the move was made to nominate a Democrat for governor who would be a strong candidate in upstate New York and help Smith gather votes—and there was one such Democrat, Franklin Roosevelt.

Smith insisted that his old friend accept the Democratic nomination for governor. Convinced that his health was improving and that he was close to being able to walk again with just a brace and a cane, Roosevelt was reluctant to leave Warm Springs. "I have had a difficult time turning down the governorship," he wrote his mother. But Smith would not take "no". To meet Franklin's terms, Herbert Lehman, a New York City banker, agreed to run for lieutenant governor and to assume much of the workload in Albany, and John J. Raskob, an influential millionaire Democrat, agreed to underwrite financing for Warm Springs.

Both Eleanor and Louis Howe advised strongly against accepting. Eleanor thought that at this point Franklin should concentrate on his recovery, and Howe felt that it would be a Republican year

October 1929! The New York Stock Exchange crash signalled the start of the Great Depression and the eventual arrival of FDR and his New Deal. Nervous patrons descended on Wall Street seeking information and reassurance from their panic-stricken brokers.

Although he was in the midst of his own campaign for New York's governorship, Roosevelt took the time to promote Al Smith's presidential campaign against Herbert C. Hoover. Here he is shown speaking at a Smith rally at Madison Square Garden in New York shortly before the election.

Police reserves were called out on October 1929, when investors thronged Wall Street, vainly seeking some information about the stock market crash. Unprecedented losses estimated at $50 billion between 1929 and 1931 paved the way for a landslide Democratic victory in the 1932 election.

anyway and that Roosevelt would lose. Finally, Roosevelt told them, "I've got to run for governor." Here again, we do not have Franklin's account of *why* he decided to stand for office. Did he really believe, rightly or wrongly, that he was close to restoring his power to walk? Or did he use this as an excuse so that Smith and his advisers would be forced to beg him, over and over again, to leave Warm Springs in order to save the Democratic Party in New York? In the end, was this the achievement Franklin had always wanted—the position that Theodore Roosevelt once held, governor of New York?

Roosevelt campaigned throughout New York by train and by car. He travelled more than 1,300

miles in one month and spoke in every county.

Frances Perkins, a close friend who was to become the first woman cabinet member in Roosevelt's presidential administration, recalled seeing Franklin being carried up a fire escape so he could speak in a rented hall. "He had accepted the ultimate humiliation which comes from being helped physically. He had accepted it smiling", she wrote. "He came up that perilous, uncomfortable, and humiliating 'entrance', and his manner was pleasant, courteous, enthusiastic. He got up in his braces, adjusted them, straightened himself, smoothed his hair, linked his arm in his son Jim's, and walked out on the platform as if there was

President Herbert Hoover, on whose shoulders fell much of the blame for the Great Depression. Hoover had defeated the Roosevelt-backed Al Smith bid for the presidency by 6.3 million votes in 1928. But when depression followed the 1929 stock market crash, Roosevelt won the 1932 election by 7 million votes over President Hoover, and carried 42 of the 48 states.

Some 12 million—out of a population of 123 million—were out of work in the United States at the height of the Depression. Thousands marched on Washington, demanding that Congress provide unemployment insurance to ease their terrible plight.

57

Even though he needed a specially equipped car to get around, FDR never let his paralysis dampen his yearning for social and outdor activity. Here he takes part in a possum hunt (he is looking at the treed animal) in 1930.

nothing unusual . . . I don't recall the speech at all. For me and for others who saw that episode his speech was less important than his courage."

Al Smith was defeated by the Republican candidate, Herbert Hoover, but Roosevelt won the governorship in New York. Smith lost New York by some 100,000 votes and Roosevelt won by only 25,000 votes out of some 4.25 million cast—Roosevelt referred to himself as the "one half of one per cent governor". But the victory quickly catapulted him into the national political arena as the best hope of the Democratic Party for winning the White House in 1932. And so, at the age of 46, Franklin Roosevelt was elected governor of New York in 1928, exactly 30 years after Theodore Roosevelt had achieved the same office.

Almost every governor of New York is a potential presidential candidate. In fact, in ten of the sixteen presidential campaigns between 1868 and 1928, a governor or former governor of New York was nominated for the presidency. Roosevelt had his sights set on the 1932 Democratic nomination and his service as governor was an apprenticeship for that.

As governor, Roosevelt obtained excellent administrative experience. He became involved in programmes for social improvement—better hospitals and mental health facilities, improved state workmen's compensation laws, and reform of the criminal justice system. Roosevelt had inherited a state government from Al Smith that was in good working order and, as governor, he continued or expanded many of the policies and programmes of his predecessor. Roosevelt seemed to love the job—

As the Depression deepened, World War I veterans increasingly insisted on being paid bonuses not due them for another few years. Throngs went to Washington in 1932 to demand them. There and in other cities, many lived in makeshift shacks, derelict cars, and packing crates on dumps and mud flats. They heaved bricks and rocks when attempts were made to evict them from their squalid "Hoovervilles" in the nation's capital.

"Whistle-stop" campaigning, criss-crossing the country by train and making speeches from the rear platform, was the custom in presidential politics (it had a brief revival in the 1984 race) prior to television. Here Herbert Hoover campaigns in 1928.

Soup kitchens sprang up across the country as the Great Depression worsened. These men are waiting in a queue for a free meal and perhaps medical attention at one such place in San Francisco in 1931.

A campaign button from Roosevelt's first run for the White House, shows the Democratic donkey putting blame for the Depression on the Republican elephant.

was poised, confident, exuberant. At that time, the governor was elected for a two-year term, and Roosevelt was easily reelected in 1930.

During the 1920s the United States was the most prosperous country in the world, its standard of living the highest. American factories produced millions of cars, refrigerators, radios, phonographs, vacuum cleaners, and all sorts of electrical devices. Wages were the highest in history. Businessmen were exalted and praised as the creators of this glowing prosperity. Profits, bigness, riches,

Roosevelt traditionally delighted in riding through the streets in an open car, brandishing his fedora and flashing his dazzling smile to cheering supporters.

optimism, success—such was the tenor of the 1920s.

In 1926 the president of the New York Stock Exchange declared that the average employee could become wealthy through stock investments: "The benefits of the capitalistic system are becoming practically universal," he boasted. Everyone, it seemed, was trying to get rich quickly. By word of mouth, by means of newspapers, the radio, and magazines, people heard of ordinary folk like themselves making fortunes in the stock market. Between 1923 and 1929 common stock prices rose almost 200 per cent. Trading increased from 236 million to 1.25 billion. Brokerage houses that traded stocks on the stock market opened new branches throughout the nation. Even William Green, the president of the American Federation of Labour, advised working men to invest. And on 4 March 1929, in his inaugural address, President Herbert Hoover declared: "I have no fear for the future of our country. It is bright with hope."

Then, in October 1929, the great economic collapse began. The prosperity of the 1920s rapidly disappeared. A sharp downward plunge of the stock market triggered a terrible contraction in the economy. There are many reasons for the economic collapse and the ensuing period known as the Great Depression. Some of the more obvious are: overproduction of consumer items, overexpansion of factories, and an unsound and unregulated financial and banking system. This led to bankruptcies, plant closings, and redundancies. By 1931, six million people were out of work, and the physical output of American manufacturing had fallen to half of what it had been in 1929. By 1932 the great car plants of Detroit operated at but 20 per cent of capacity, the massive steel plants of Pittsburgh at 12 per cent. The hard-earned savings of many average persons were rapidly exhausted. A new class of Americans appeared—the hungry.

Part of FDR's undeniable charm was his ability to put others at ease. Here he makes light of his crippled legs, perhaps to alleviate any unease on behalf of the observers, as he hauls himself out of his limousine for a major speech in 1932 at the Hollywood Bowl.

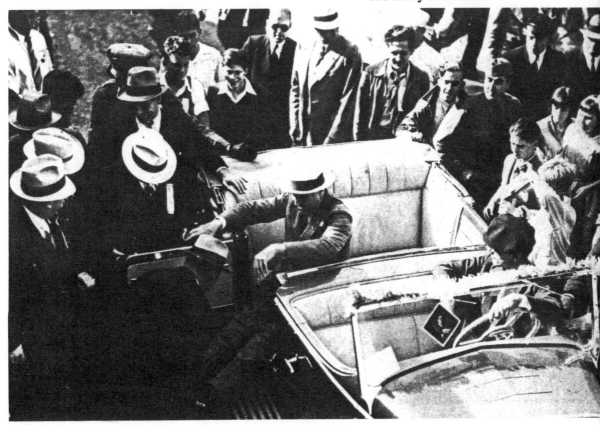

6

New Hope for the Nation

The 1932 presidential election came in the midst of the greatest economic depression experienced by the American people. Never before in the history of the United States had pessimism been so universal. The descent from the height of prosperity of the late 1920s had been rapid, bringing fear and uncertainty. By March 1932 approximately twelve million men and women were unemployed. By March 1933 unemployment had reached 13.5 million. In the hard-hit cities, long queues of hungry people waited before charity soup kitchens for something to eat, and thousands, unable to pay rent, huddled in empty lots. Homeless people made shelters out of old packing cartons. Others waited in line to sift through rubbish in search of something to eat. Infant mortality jumped. Death due to starvation became a new category for the New York City Board of Health. A million or more Americans wandered aimlessly throughout the country looking for work.

President Herbert Hoover had tried to use governmental power to check the economic downfall but without success. Critics of Hoover claimed that

Roosevelt pressed Congress to get his New Deal into gear as soon as he was inaugurated. More vital legislation was passed in his first term than in any other four years of U.S. history. Here a political cartoon depicts FDR whiplashing a sluggish Congress.

Like his predecessors since the start of the railway age, Roosevelt did his share of "whistle-stop" campaigning. Here he shares the rear platform of his special train with John N. ("Texas Jack") Garner (1868–1967), who was FDR's first vice-president.

The infectious Roosevelt laugh. The president guffaws as Will Rogers, noted for the political bite of his humour, jokes at a Los Angeles microphone in 1932. Between them are Roosevelt's son James, William G. McAdoo (1863-1941), who was President Wilson's son-in-law and secretary of the treasury, and James Farley, FDR's campaign manager.

his policies were too conservative and lacked imagination. His defenders maintained that, regardless of the president's efforts, the depression just had to run its course. But millions of Americans could not afford to wait for the economic system to correct itself. The depression had caused not only financial disaster but also, and perhaps more important, a loss in personal pride, status, and sense of self-respect. Many Americans demanded prompt and immediate action. As a result, all indications pointed to a sweeping Democratic victory in the 1932 presidential election.

The Republicans knew that their position was weak indeed. But they renominated Hoover and campaigned on his record. The Democrats met in

Front page of *The New York Times*, announcing Roosevelt's election in 1932. His landslide victory also carried the Democrats—most of whom favoured the repeal of the Prohibition Amendment—into control of both houses of Congress.

Typescript of Roosevelt's first inaugural address, 4 March 1933: "Let me assert my firm belief that the only thing we have to fear is fear itself—nameless, unreasoning, unjustified terror which paralyzes needed efforts to convert retreat into advance."

Chicago in June, confident of victory. After a successful pre-convention, masterfully managed by James Farley and Louis Howe, Franklin Roosevelt won the Democratic nomination on the fourth ballot. The 50-year-old governor broke with tradition by flying to the convention to accept the nomination in person. "I pledge you," he told the delegates, "I pledge myself, to a new deal for the American people."

Roosevelt toured the nation talking about economic reforms. He declared his total support for the system of capitalism but insisted that changes were needed to prevent dangerous revolutionary movements from developing out of the economic collapse. Hoover, on the other hand, opposed proposals for additional federal controls and stressed his belief that voluntary cooperation of individuals would restore prosperity. There was only one campaign issue—the economic depression.

On Election Day, 1932, the nation gave Roosevelt a smashing victory—22,809,038 votes to Hoover's 15,758,901. Hoover carried only six states, losing the electoral vote 472 to 59. The Democrats also elected heavy majorities to both houses of Congress. "This is the greatest night of my life!" Roosevelt declared on hearing the election results. Later that evening, as his son James helped him into bed, the same bed in which he had lain nearly

A man comes to wisdom in many years of public life. He knows well that when the light of favour shines upon him, it comes not, of necessity, that he himself is important. Favour comes because for a brief moment in the great space of human change and progress some general human purpose finds in him a satisfactory embodiment.
—FRANKLIN ROOSEVELT
speaking on the campaign trail in 1932

helpless after his polio attack, the president-elect turned to his son and said:

"You know, Jimmy, all my life I have been afraid of only one thing—fire. Tonight I think I'm afraid of something else."

"Afraid of what, Pa?"

"I'm afraid that I may not have the strength to do this job."

He then asked his son to pray for him.

The American nation wanted a change and they

A "Hooverville" of the unemployed—a hodgepodge of flimsy huts made from scraps of junk—in New York's Central Park during the Great Depression.

placed their faith in Franklin Delano Roosevelt.

Between Election Day and the swearing in of the new president, the depression worsened. Numerous bank failures, the result of sudden panic by depositors, added to the growing alarm—over 5,000 banks had been forced to close, with a loss of more than $3.4 billion to depositors. By 4 March 1933, the day of the inauguration, banks were closed in all but two states. The financial crisis was at its worst point. Stock and grain markets were shut.

As a consistent part of a clear policy, the United States is following a twofold neutrality toward any and all Nations which engage in wars that are not of immediate concern to the Americas. First, we decline to encourage the prosecution of war by permitting belligerents to obtain arms . . . from the United States. Second, we seek to discourage the use by belligerent Nations of any and all American products calculated to facilitate the prosecution of a war in quantities over and above our normal exports of them in time of peace.
—FRANKLIN ROOSEVELT
speaking in 1936

They seek — this minority in business and industry — to control and often do control and use for their own purposes legitimate and highly honoured business associations; they engage in vast propaganda to spread fear and discord among the people — they would 'gang up' against the people's liberties
—FRANKLIN ROOSEVELT

FDR's cabinet met for the first time on 5 March 1933. Seated clockwise from the president are William H. Woodin (treasury), Homer S. Cummings (attorney general), Claude Swanson (navy), Henry Wallace (agriculture), Frances Perkins (labour), Daniel C. Roper (commerce), Harold L. Ickes (interior), James A. Farley (postmaster general), George H. Dern (war), and Cordell Hull (state). Of these, Ickes, Perkins, and Hull were the most influential in shaping New Deal policy.

Marches on Washington were a major part of the Depression scene. On one such march in 1932, 10,000 marched from Pennsylvania to besiege the Capitol and ask Congress and President Hoover for aid. Roosevelt declined White House invitations to discuss the situation, and refused to help until such time as he took office.

Business lay stagnant. Hunger marchers paraded in New York City and Chicago as if in a ghastly mockery of the official ceremonies in Washington. It seemed that all the fears brought on by the depression had come to a climax.

Roosevelt's inaugural address gave hope to a disillusioned America. His assured tone and absolute confidence in recovery provided a needed tonic to a confused nation. The new president's encouraging voice urged immediate steps to end unemployment, to aid the farmer, and to bring about national recovery. If Congress failed to act, he promised to seek broad powers "to wage a war against the emergency, as great as the power that would be given to me if we were in fact invaded by a foreign foe."

This vigorous assertion of national leadership, combined with Roosevelt's forceful presentation, inspired confidence and renewed faith in the democratic system of government. Not since George Washington had a president started his term of office with such popular support.

In Franklin Roosevelt's first term (1933-37) the nation saw more important legislation passed than in any other four years in American history. Roosevelt and his advisers — called the "brain trust" — believed that immediate federal action was needed to restore confidence in the economic system. Their goal was to maintain capitalism but, at the same time, to reform, not destroy, the economic system that had brought hardship to so many.

Roosevelt was also strongly committed to the idea of humane government, one that would consider the basic needs of the people. He was not restricted by any dogma or rigid philosophy of government. Rather, he was practical and experimental in trying to rebuild the shattered economy. His programmes were many and varied. "Do something," he said. "If it works, do it some more. And if it does not work, then do something else."

Roosevelt exuded confidence. His optimism and self-assurance were conveyed in a series of radio addresses which came to be known as "the fireside chats". There were about 30 such broadcasts during his twelve years in office and millions of people eagerly awaited each one. "My friends," he would begin, and then, in simple but eloquent language, he would explain his New Deal. His warm personality, his sense of personal concern, and his informality combined to make these talks a success. He spoke as though he were actually sitting on a front porch with his neighbours. Eleanor Roosevelt later observed that after her husband's death, people would stop her on the street to say "they missed the way the president used to talk to them. They'd say: 'He used to talk to me about my government.' There was a real dialogue between Franklin and the people," she wrote.

The first fireside chat, a few days after he took office, dealt with the banking and financial crisis. After discussing his programme—a four-day national banking holiday—Roosevelt asked the public to

World War I veterans who participated in the 1932 Bonus March on Washington rest on the steps of the capital while the House of Representatives debates legislation to give them payments to ease their Depression-spawned poverty and misfortune.

Roosevelt's New Deal brought an "alphabet soup" of new agencies: NRA, WPA, TVA, etc. One, the Federal Employment Relief Administration (FERA) even established a class to teach the unemployed the basics of "washing" for gold when some of the precious metal was found in a Denver stream in 1934.

I have sympathy with President Roosevelt because he marches straight to his objective over Congress, over lobbies, over stubborn bureaucracies.

—ADOLF HITLER
chancellor of Nazi Germany,
speaking in 1933

share their views with him—and the White House received thousands of letters from ordinary people who were convinced that the president was willing to listen. And he did. Many of the letters simply told of the listeners' faith in his leadership.

The most pressing and immediate problem when Roosevelt took office was to feed the millions of the hungry. The Federal Emergency Relief Administration (FERA) in 1933 provided immediate federal grants to the states to assist the most needy with money. When this proved inadequate, the President established the Civilian Works Administration (CWA), which between November 1933 and April 1934 put some six million people to work on specially created jobs. These jobs—such as road maintenance and the building of playgrounds, parks, sewers, and airports—were not to compete with private business but to create public projects to employ the unemployed.

Another agency created in 1933, the Public Works Administration (PWA), planned bridges, dams, hospitals, and other public projects. The PWA contracted and paid private companies to do the work. All construction contracts awarded by the PWA required the hiring of some black workers. This set a precedent for other federal agencies. Among PWA's many achievements were the Triborough Bridge in New York City, a new sewage system in Chicago, a municipal auditorium in Kansas City, and a new water-supply system in Denver.

In 1935 most relief programmes—that is, programmes to help the unemployed—were launched under a new agency, the Works Progress Administration (WPA). The WPA attempted to make use of an individual's skill, whether it be sewing or translating books into Braille. At its peak in November 1938, nearly 3.3 million persons were on its payroll. When the WPA ended in 1941, it had provided work for a total of 8 million people.

Among its 250,000 projects, the WPA had built or improved more than 2,500 hospitals, 5,900 school buildings, 1,000 airports, and nearly 13,000 playgrounds. Some called these make-work programmes a "boondoggle"—a waste of money. But people were going back to work. And their salaries, besides giving them the ability to buy things, also helped to stimulate the depressed economy.

The WPA also gave employment to artists, musicians, actors, singers, and writers. After all, Roosevelt said, they have to eat too. Some of the WPA cultural projects included interviews with more than 2,000 surviving ex-slaves and the recording of folk tunes, American Indian songs, and black spirituals. On post office walls around the country, WPA artists painted murals, "Some of it good," observed Roosevelt, "some of it not so good, but all of it natural, human, eager, and alive."

Hundreds of WPA teachers taught painting, pottery, weaving, and carving. Americans who had never seen a live play or concert came to federal theatre performances. In four years, the Federal Theatre Project, a division of the WPA, produced over 2,700 plays, including the classics, children's plays, new American plays, and dance dramas. All in all, more than thirty million Americans saw at one time or another a WPA theatre production.

Another New Deal programme for helping the unemployed was the Civilian Conservation Corps (CCC). Between 1933 and 1941 the CCC took some 2.7 million young men between the ages of 18 and 25 and hired them to work on erosion control, tree planting, forest-fire fighting, dam construction, mosquito control, and other such projects. The corps also improved beaches and national and state parks. Recruited mainly from the cities where it was almost impossible for a young man to find a job, members lived in camps built by the War

The National Recovery Administration, which in 1934 authorized collective bargaining by labour and established a three-billion-dollar public works programme, was regarded as the mainspring of the New Deal. Until it was declared unconstitutional, the NRA insignia with the eagle appeared everywhere. There was even a popular song called "The Blue Eagle".

Henry Ford was one of the many industrial leaders who opposed NRA. Known for his fierce individualism, Ford strongly opposed FDR's economic policies, which he felt represented an intrusion by government into the workings of the free enterprise system.

Department. Of the $30 a month wages received, $22 was sent to the young man's family. The CCC became a popular programme which bolstered the morale of many young unemployed.

Young people were also assisted by the National Youth Administration (NYA). This agency paid more than 500,000 college students to do part-time work, whether in libraries or as research aides. Another 1.5 million high school students received similar aid, usually enough to enable the student to remain in school and off the labour market. The aim of both the CCC and the NYA, in addition to helping young people, was to try to prevent them from adding to the ranks of the unemployed.

No part of the New Deal drew more criticism than did these relief programmes. Although their cost was enormous, they gave many people the sense that their government cared about them. While less than half of the total unemployed were ever involved in these relief programmes, the overwhelming majority of Americans supported the president's bold attempt to control the unemployment problem. Never before in American history had any presidential administration shown such concern. To many, Franklin Roosevelt became a personal hero.

While the income of most Americans increased during the 1920s, that of the farmers greatly declined. The basic problem was that they grew more food than the nation could consume. The settlement of the Great Plains, which put millions of acres of new land under cultivation, various inventions such as the motorized tractor and the

President Roosevelt endorses the Social Security Bill on 14 August 1935, surrounded by members of Congress. The woman behind FDR is Labour Secretary Frances Perkins, the first woman cabinet member. Enactment of the radical new programme elicited charges of "socialism" from some of FDR's more conservative detractors.

Representatives of the arts and culture were no less hard hit by the ravages of the Great Depression than were the unemployed workers. Here a contingent of New York City's "Destitute Artists of Greenwich Village" is encamped in Washington.

In the wake of two terrible droughts in 1934 and 1936, a tide of migrant farmers, their once fertile fields now dust-beaten and barren, headed westward in search of kindlier climates. Known as "Okies", these unfortunate families had to rely totally on casual labour or some sort of local assistance to survive.

harvester, and new and better techniques of insect control all enabled the farmer to grow more and more. But in agriculture, the law of supply and demand ruled—that is, prices for farm goods were determined by quantity and demand. Because there was too large a food supply, farm prices dropped dramatically. Farmers left their crops in the fields to rot. Some used their grain as fuel—at least it was cheaper than coal. Others just abandoned their farms or were evicted because they had no money to pay their bills or meet their mortgage payments.

Hence Roosevelt faced a contradiction—while people in the cities were going hungry, food was being destroyed on the farms. While fruit was left to rot on the trees, hunger marchers paraded in front of the White House demanding something to eat.

In 1933 Roosevelt and his advisers contrived the Agricultural Adjustment Act (AAA), which, with some modifications, is still in effect today. The AAA raised farm prices by paying farmers to cut back production. Farmers were also paid if they did not use a portion of their land. To cut food production

"Darkness was coming in at 3 o'clock", begins this letter from a victim of the winds that struck the "Dust Bowl" in 1935, destroying farmland and forcing a migration of farmers to the Pacific Coast states.

Rolla Kansas, May. 6-35
Mr, Franklin. D. Roosevelt. Washington
D.C. Dear Mr, Roosevelt. we are mailing
you a picture of the dust storm which came
April 14-35 This was a North east wind and
Darkness came ... When this hit us ...
The Sun was Shining bright and,
Darkness was coming on at 3.0clo
in the evening. Taken from the water
tower one Hundred feet high.
Yours Truly
Chas. P. Williams
Rolla Kansas,

Dust storm in Kansas Apr. 14 1935

In the Southwest and Midwest, severe dust storms in the mid-1930s gave many farmers yet another burden to add to the Depression problems they shared with the rest of the country. Many even wrote letters to the president, seeking help against the swirling winds that blew the topsoil from once-productive fields.

Our economic life today is a seamless web. We cannot have independence . . . unless we take full account of our interdependence in order to provide a balanced economic well-being for every citizen. . . . This nation cannot endure if it is half "boom" and half "broke."
–FRANKLIN ROOSEVELT
speaking in 1932

when people were hungry seemed a terrible thing to do. This contradiction between the government's programme of controlling food abundance and the reality of millions of Americans suffering from a lack of food was never resolved. In fact, it remains a problem today. For the farmers, the AAA worked. Prices for their goods rose and even many of the most conservative farmers came to regard Roosevelt as a saviour.

One of the poorest of all American farm areas was the Tennessee River valley. To provide the basic benefits of electricity to this depressed area, President Roosevelt in 1933 asked Congress to create the Tennessee Valley Authority (TVA). The TVA eventually built fifteen more dams both to control river flooding and to create cheap electric power. States affected by the TVA were parts of Virginia, North Carolina, South Carolina, Kentucky, Alabama, Georgia, and Tennessee. While some saw the TVA as a threat to private enterprise, most Americans viewed it as a bold and original way of handling one of the nation's most serious regional problems.

For the troubled business community, in 1933 the New Deal created the Federal Deposit Insurance Corporation (FDIC), which functions to this day. The FDIC guaranteed bank deposits so that people were assured by the government of the security of their personal savings and other capital. This stopped such problems as nationwide financial panic and the subsequent default of banks. The Securities and Exchange Commission (SEC), also still in operation, registered all securities traded on stock

> *The simple fact of our dependence upon each other was either unknown or entirely ignored by the Republican leadership of the postwar period. Their doctrine was to give definite help at the top and to utter pious hopes for the bottom. Twelve years of that brought the inevitable crash.*
> —FRANKLIN ROOSEVELT
> speaking in 1932

Diablo Dam on the Skagit River in the state of Washington. This hydroelectric installation is an impressive example of the many public works projects undertaken by the Roosevelt administration in its effort to provide employment during the Depression.

Many of the public works projects spawned by the New Deal (such as this generating plant) were geared to meet regional needs.

BACK TO 1929

ROOSEVELT IS A RED!

G.O.P.

WALL ST.

With revolutionary New Deal legislation being enacted at a feverish pace during FDR's first two years in office many die-hard Republicans were not reticent about attaching the "communist" label to the president's political philosophy. Ironically, it was to a large extent through Roosevelt's efforts that the economic system of which Republicans were so enamoured—corporate capitalism—was rectified and restored.

exchanges. Full and accurate information about a corporation had to be supplied to stock buyers, Roosevelt appointed as its first chairman Joseph Kennedy (the father of President John F. Kennedy).

The National Recovery Act (NRA) was not as successful. Hailed by Roosevelt as the "most important and far-reaching legislation ever enacted", it failed in its attempt to ration the nation's business among the country's surviving corporations. This was to be accomplished through a series of "codes of fair competition". While the NRA failed in many of its objectives, it did have some success. Codes of fair competition in the textile industry, for example, raised wages from $5 per week for most workers to a minimum of $12 to $13. The NRA established the principle of maximum hours and minimum wages on a national basis for the first time. It also outlawed child labour. But the NRA was too complex and involved too much paperwork. (Ultimately, this type of business regulation through codes was declared unconstitutional by the Supreme Court in 1935.)

Most of the New Deal's famous "alphabet agencies"—PWA, CCC, SEC, AAA, TVA, NRA, and FDIC—became law during the first 100 days of Roosevelt's administration. Hope seemed to have surfaced everywhere. The president was enormously popular. The people had demanded action from their leaders and Roosevelt had responded with bold new initiatives. Indeed, Roosevelt and his administration had changed the centre of power in the United States in that more power was given to the national government and to the president in particular. Though Roosevelt vastly expanded presidential involvement in the process of government, the balances of power—a basic tenet of the American political system—survived. No industry was nationalized, and the profit motive still prevailed.

The fear that the president had tried to interfere with America's "free enterprise" was unwarranted. Without the immediate resolve of Roosevelt, without the programmes that tried to feed and employ the people, the business community might have collapsed. In the 1934 congressional elections the

Democrats scored overwhelming victories, swelling their majorities in both the House and the Senate. This landslide for the Democrats could only be interpreted as a ringing endorsement for the policies of Franklin Roosevelt.

Still, some insisted the president had moved too fast with his programmes—that change was too rapid, that the business world was being disrupted and dominated. Others said that he was not moving fast enough in alleviating the problems of the poor. As criticism for not doing enough to help those at the bottom of the economic ladder increased, Roosevelt moved resolutely for more reform.

In 1935 the Social Security Act was passed. For the first time, the federal government, using employer and employee contributions, made payments for pensions to the aged and the ill. Unemployment insurance began and workers who lost their jobs could now collect payments while looking for new work. In the same year Congress passed the Wagner Act. This legislation guaranteed collective bargaining and prohibited employer interference with union-organizing activities. It also provided that representatives of the majority of the employees in any factory could be the exclusive bargaining representatives for *all* the employees in contact negotiations. Workers were no longer negotiating alone, but in mass. Indeed, the Wagner Act caused an enormous expansion of unions with ensuing bloody conflicts between employees and employers.

In an effort to prevent union organization, General Motors spent almost $1 million on "goon squads" to harass workers through intimidation. Virtual warfare took place as unions attempted to organize the car and steel industries. Despite the antagonism of big business, organized labour continued to grow.

On the other hand, the U.S. Supreme Court began to rule some of the New Deal acts, such as the NRA, unconstitutional. The big test for Roosevelt and the New Deal would be the presidential election of 1936. Voters could then describe if they agreed with his policies, and if they should give the president a second term.

The New Deal-sponsored "Mobilization for Human Needs" encouraged individual Americans to do whatever they could to combat the Depression. This poster encouraged local drives for funds to be used directly by the communities raising the money.

Joseph P. Kennedy (1888–1969), the father of President John F. Kennedy (1917–1963), was chosen by FDR to be the first head of the Securities and Exchange Commission (SEC). Later the two men had a falling out because of Kennedy's soft attitude toward the Nazis in the 1930s.

7
Thunder on the Right

In 1936 Franklin Roosevelt was at the height of his popularity. His vigorous reform policies, his frontal attack on depression conditions, made him a sure winner for a second term. Many millions felt that their personal lot had been improved by the New Deal. However, he was criticized by conservatives—his old Groton schoolmates, for example, thought Roosevelt was a traitor to his economic class and at Harvard's 300th anniversary celebration in 1936, undergraduates booed him. He also faced the objections of radicals who though the capitalist system should be replaced with a more responsive one. Roosevelt seemed serenely confident that the nation was on its way to a full economic recovery. In four years the New Deal had stimulated the economy. It had relieved distress on the farms. It had helped the unemployed. "Of course we will continue to seek to improve working conditions for the workers of America," he declared. "Of course, we will continue to work for cheaper electricity in the homes and on the farms of America . . . Of course we will continue our efforts for young men and women . . . for the crippled, for the blind, for the mothers, our insurance for the unemployed, our security for the aged . . . For these things, too, and for a multitude of things like them, we have only just begun to fight." Indeed, Roosevelt the patrician had become Roosevelt the hero of the lower class.

We have a clear mandate . . . that Americans must forswear that conception of the acquisition of wealth which, through excessive profits, creates undue private power over private affairs and, to our misfortune, over public affairs as well.
—FRANKLIN ROOSEVELT
speaking in 1935

In 1936 Alfred M. Landon of Kansas lost the presidential election to Roosevelt by eleven million votes, managing to carry only Maine and Vermont.

Roosevelt with Blaze, his son's pet which caused a storm of criticism when it was part of a military escort during World War II. FDR was a lover of dogs. His most famous dog, Fala, was a Scottish terrier that he immortalized in 1940 campaign speeches.

As First Lady, Eleanor Roosevelt kept up a whirlwind pace that almost rivalled her husband's. Here she leaves a coal mine after examining working conditions she found deplorable.

We know now that government by organized money is just as dangerous as government by organized mob. Never before have these forces been so united against one candidate as they stand today. They are unanimous in their hate for me—and I welcome their hatred.

—FRANKLIN ROOSEVELT
speaking in 1936

The Republicans attacked every aspect of the New Deal. "America is in peril. The welfare of American men and women and the future of our youth are at stake," were the words that began their 1936 platform. For president, the Republicans nominated Governor Alfred M. Landon of Kansas. The Republicans, with "Oh, Susannah" as their campaign song, appealed to nostalgia for an older, more simple day. Landon claimed that Roosevelt had ruined the country—that he was Franklin Deficit Roosevelt; that Roosevelt had disregarded the Constitution; that he had created big government at the expense of liberty. The Republicans hoped that Landon's unpretentious small town manner would be a pleasant relief from Roosevelt's Harvard accent and from his polished campaign style. They were wrong!

The Democrats renominated Roosevelt by acclamation. Veteran reporters and politicians who accompanied Roosevelt on his nationwide campaign trip were startled by the response of the vast crowds that turned out to see him. Many carried homemade signs: "He saved my Home"; He gave me a Job"; "Roosevelt my Hero"; "Roosevelt is my Friend". Wild enthusiasm greeted the president in what became a triumphal procession rather than a campaign trip. In Detroit, for example, Roosevelt spoke from the steps of the city hall to a monumental mass of people. Even at small towns where the campaign train did not stop—it would whiz by at 40 to 60 miles an hour—hundreds of people gathered to shout "We want Roosevelt".

One veteran reporter wrote of the president's reception in Jersey City: "From the moment that the progression of cars rolled out of the Holland Tunnel the thunder assaulted the ear, and the whole city, under a cloudless blue sky, seemed one mass of flag-waving humanity." Chicago, he reported, gave Roosevelt an even more impressive welcome:

As the country slowly recovered from the Depression, organized labour, despite enjoying the strongest presidential backing it had ever had, became restless. The General Motors strike of 1937 provoked a major crisis. Here members of the "Women's Emergency Brigade" pose with clubs used to break windows at a GM Chevrolet plant in Flint, Michigan. Surprisingly, Roosevelt did not involve himself to a great degree in the labour conflicts that often beset his presidency.

"In the early evening the President rode for five miles in an open car through streets so crowded that only a narrow lane was left. Despite the protests of the Secret Service, people had been allowed to swarm off the curbs and it was all the motorcycle police could do to force a way through for the presidential cavalcade.

"This was King Crowd. They were out to have a large time and they had it. Every kind of band—bagpipers, piano accordions, jazz, fife-and-drum, bugle corps—lined the narrow lane of humanity through which the presidential party passed. As the parade turned off Michigan Boulevard into West Madison Street the mass of people became denser and noisier. They shrieked from rooftops; they sang and danced; they leaned from tenement windows . . . And all the time a rain of torn paper fluttered down, like grey snow in the half-lighted streets."

Throughout the campaign, Roosevelt never abandoned his theme: He was the champion of the "forgotten man".

During the Depression the federal government purchased surplus crops so as to help the suffering farmers. The foodstuffs were distributed to the unemployed and needy. Here, potatoes and cabbage are given to Cleveland residents, nearly 100,000 of whom were on some form of governmental relief.

On Election Day, 1936, American voters gave Roosevelt a clear mandate—the president carried all but two states, Maine and Vermont. His 27.7 million votes represented 60 per cent of the total votes cast. In the cities, his margin shattered all records. Political writers searched for sufficiently descriptive words with which to convey the sheer scale of Roosevelt's landslide victory—"an avalanche", "a tornado", "a tidal wave". One reporter noted that if Roosevelt "were to say a kind word for the man-eating shark, people would look thoughtful and say perhaps there are two sides to the question." "He has been all but crowned by the people," declared another.

On inaugural day, 1937, Franklin D. Roosevelt could look at a multitude of faces less drawn and anxious than four years earlier. The New Deal had passed a bewildering number of laws and had created dozens of agencies to meet the problems of relief, recovery, and reform. Although these policies did not completely end depression conditions, hope had returned to America. Unemployment was reduced. Farm prices rose dramatically—corn sold at $1.26 a bushel compared with 24¢ in 1933. Weekly factory wages increased an estimated 65 per cent. In some quarters, though, the New Deal policies of positive government and increased taxes to pay for these programmes aroused deep bitterness. The people as a whole, however, had more income than at any time since the depression first struck the country.

Roosevelt delivered his second inaugural address on 20 January 1937. He declared that his programme of social reform was by no means complete. In 1933 his prime objective had been recovery—his new objective was to achieve consolidation of what had been accomplished plus an extension of the New Deal's social and economic programmes. "In this nation," he said, "I see tens of millions of its citizens—a substantial part of its whole population—who at this very moment are denied the greater part of what the very lowest standards of living today call the necessities of life . . . I see one-third of a nation ill-housed, ill-clad, ill-nourished."

I should like to have it said of my first administration that in it the forces of selfishness and of lust for power met their match. I should like to have it said of my second administration that in it these forces met their master.
—FRANKLIN ROOSEVELT
speaking in 1936

Frances Perkins was the first woman named to a presidential cabinet post. FDR appointed her secretary of labour in 1933.

But Roosevelt saw these bleak conditions as a challenge. "It is not in despair that I paint you that picture, I paint it for you in hope—because the nation seeing and understanding the injustice of it, proposes to paint it out."

Before attacking these problems, however, Roosevelt set out to neutralize a major obstacle to his reform vision—the U.S. Supreme Court. During the 1936 campaign he had challenged his conservative opponents—"economic royalists", he called them. Despite his smashing election victory, the economic royalists would have the upper hand so long as the Supreme Court continued to declare New Deal laws unconstitutional. Roosevelt believed that he had a mandate from the people to go forward with his programmes. But first he had to do something about the obstructionist Supreme Court.

By tradition, the Supreme Court is usually the most conservative branch of the federal government. And the Court, by following a narrow interpretation of the Constitution, had invalidated several important New Deal measures. Franklin Roosevelt believed that the 1936 election had given him a clear mandate from the people to go forward with his reform policies. But how could he if the Court would judge these programmes illegal? The Social Security Act and the Wagner Act, for example, were due for review—what would happen if these acts failed the judicial test? How could conditions for the "forgotten man"—the person at the bottom of the economic ladder—be improved if the Court stood in the way of change?

In February 1937, barely three weeks after his second inauguration, Roosevelt proposed a sweeping Court revision plan. The president would be empowered to appoint an additional Court justice for every member who had reached the age of 70 and chose not to retire at full salary within six months. Since six justices were over 70—including four of the Court's most conservative ones—Roosevelt would be able to appoint enough pro-New Deal justices to ensure favourable Court review of his programmes. There was nothing illegal about this proposal. Most industries and even the federal

Supreme Court Justice Hugo Black (1886–1971) of Alabama. His support in Congress of Roosevelt's New Deal policies gained him a controversial appointment to the court after FDR's attempt to "pack" the tribunal failed. Ironically, Black, who admitted to having once been a member of the Ku Klux Klan, was criticized for being too much of a liberal.

civil service and the military have some type of mandatory retirement requirement. And the number of Supreme Court justices had changed several times—the Constitution makes no mention of the size of the Court. But the present number of nine had *seemed* almost unholy to tamper with it. To conservatives, both Democratic and Republican, Roosevelt had gone too far. The president had struck a tender nerve. Cries of "dictator" were raised. Tampering with the Court brought howls of criticism.

Several events led to a bruising defeat for Roosevelt. The Supreme Court, by a narrow 5 to 4 vote, upheld a key New Deal labour agency. Then, one of the most conservative justices chose to retire, thus giving Roosevelt the right to appoint his successor.

The president had suffered a humiliating defeat by raising controversy, splitting the Democratic party as a result of this controversy, and then being embarrassed by both a dramatic reverse in the Court justices' attitudes, and a failure to arouse support for his plan in Congress. This battle was the beginning of the end for New Deal reforms, despite the resounding 1936 election victory.

In the end, however, while Roosevelt might have lost his battle with the Supreme Court, and his plan

After the Supreme Court had ruled unconstitutional several parts of his New Deal legislation, Roosevelt proposed, unsuccessfully, to add six more members to the Court, thus assuring him a favourable majority. This is a formal portrait of the "Nine Old Men" taken after the "packing" move backfired on Roosevelt.

Roosevelt's 1937 plan to "pack" the Supreme Court to overcome its right-wing tendencies provoked a storm of criticism throughout the country. A contemporary cartoon emphasizes surprise at the widespread opposition to his plan.

ALL I SAID WAS 'GIMME SIX MORE JUSTICES!'

Roosevelt's battle with private-power interests climaxed in the fight over the Tennessee Valley Authority. The right of TVA, a government agency, to compete with privately owned companies was eventually upheld by the Supreme Court. Its opponents criticized the project as socialist but customers in the area served welcomed TVA.

Violence broke out in 1937 when Henry Ford used his private police force to block strikers at his Michigan car plants. Walter Reuther (1907–1970) (left), president of the United Auto Workers (UAW), shown with another union official, was badly beaten along with several associates when they tried to distribute pamphlets at a Ford motor plant.

died in the Senate Judiciary Committee, he won the war. Within the next few years six other ageing justices retired and Roosevelt was able to remake the court in his image through the appointment of liberal jurists.

To understand why the New Deal came to an end during Roosevelt's second term, one must understand Roosevelt and the Democratic Party. When Roosevelt came to office in 1933, the Democratic Party had not been in power since 1921. Hundreds of political jobs had to be filled by the president. In addition, the many New Deal agencies and bureaus needed people to run them. Roosevelt was a master politician, and what held the New Deal together during his first term was not a common ideology shared by all Democrats, but Roosevelt's skilful use of patronage, or political appointments.

The United States has two major political parties, but within these parties are considerable differences of opinion on almost every issue. Roosevelt, however, through his patronage power, was able to unite the Democratic Party behind his programmes for handling the nation's economic crisis. It is not that all Democrats suddenly favoured the AAA or the TVA or social security; but Roosevelt, the politician, was able to forge unity through his skilful use of patronage. Politicians thrive on the work done for them by others—those who run the

campaigns, those who give the supporting speeches, those who get out the vote on election day. Patronage jobs are the rewards that politicians can offer in return for loyal service. And thousands of such jobs in his administration were used by Roosevelt to obtain the necessary support for his programmes. There is nothing illegal about this — in fact, it is a tactic as old as the institution of political parties.

In his second term Roosevelt wanted to move more rapidly towards his social and economic goals, faster than a majority of the Democratic Party were willing to follow. That is, there was general harmony among Democrats and his patronage assisted this harmony — during the first term. In the second term, however, many conservative Democrats were saying "enough", let us wait and see the results of our programmes before going forward with more. Some conservative Democrats even argued that Roosevelt's programmes seemed a betrayal of the American pioneer tradition of self-reliance — that social security and the WPA were socialist and were turning the country into a welfare state in which

TVA, despite the storm it aroused, brought integrated development to the entire Tennessee basin.

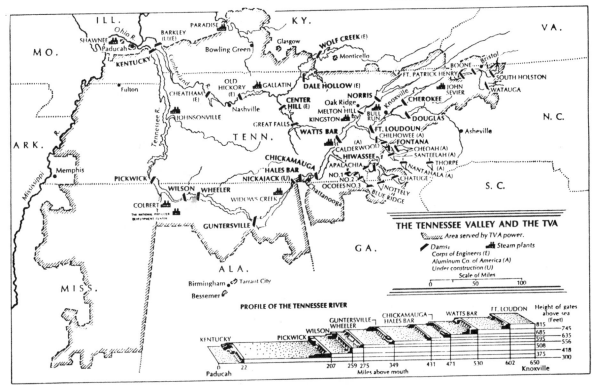

In 1939 striking miners shut down the nation's coal mines. Here United Mine Workers president John L.Lewis (1880–1969) (left) and another union leader confer with Labour Secretary Frances Perkins on ways to end the strike. Lewis later broke with the American Federation of Labor (AF of L) to form the more radical Congress of Industrial Organizations (CIO).

personal lives were being regimented by the government. Roosevelt, though, embraced the liberal wing of the Democratic Party and wanted to move forward using the gains of his first term as the stepping-stone towards further reform. But he was losing his grip on many of his fellow Democrats. Hence, the Democratic Party split during Roosevelt's second term. The president's triumph in 1936, rather than giving harmony to the Democratic Party, brought the party much discord.

Roosevelt's striking defeat on the Supreme Court issue widened the split within the Democratic

Norman Thomas (1884–1968), the Socialist Party leader, ran unsuccessfully for president six times between 1928 and 1948. He repeatedly accused FDR of bolstering a failed economic system, one that Thomas felt needed total reform.

Party. Ideology, not patronage, now seemed to dominate Congress. Had the New Deal gone too far? Was the Wagner Act contributing to labour violence? Were the programmes of the first administration really working? Was relief becoming a permanent way of life? And, above all, how far would Roosevelt go to assist the nation's "ill-housed", "ill-clad" and "ill-nourished"?—the underprivileged one-third of the population?

Some of the president's programmes did reach fruition in his second term. The U.S. Housing Authority, for example, was established to make long-term, low-interest loans to state and city public housing agencies to encourage the clearing of slums and the building of new housing. As the political climate of the world began to change, however, the need to do something for the poor seemed less urgent. And crises in Europe and Asia engrossed the president's energy and overshadowed domestic programmes and problems.

The shepherd drives the wolf from the sheep's throat, for which the sheep thanks the shepherd as his liberator, while the wolf denounces him for the same act, as the destroyer of liberty.... Plainly, the sheep and the wolf are not agreed upon a definition of the word liberty.
—FRANKLIN ROOSEVELT
speaking in 1936

Two of the most vocal of Roosevelt haters—there were many of them—were a Catholic priest, Charles Coughlin (1891–1979), and a Protestant minister, Gerald L. K. Smith. Both were extreme right wingers who gained large national followings with angry radio denunciations of FDR.

8
The War for Survival

Throughout the 1930s the United States clung to an isolationist foreign policy, believing that even if war began abroad, the nation should remain neutral and not get involved. The bitter memories of World War I and the dread of a future war helped to create a public opinion that earnestly searched for peace and avoided war. Even during the Spanish Civil War (1936–39), which saw a republican form of government overwhelmed by fascist forces, the Roosevelt administration supported a total arms embargo, despite the fact that it severely hurt the Spanish republic's cause. Likewise, during 1937 and 1938 public opinion overwhelmingly opposed relaxing immigration laws. As a result, Roosevelt felt himself virtually powerless to aid Germany's 500,000 persecuted Jews. But the European events of 1939, climaxing with the German invasion of Poland, convinced many Americans that their own interests were threatened deeply by foreign developments and that perhaps they could not afford to remain still.

The situation in Europe had been heading towards a crisis, and on 1 September 1939, war broke out. According to a Gallup Poll in the United States 82 per cent favoured an Allied victory and only 2 per cent supported Nazi Germany. But feeling in America was almost unanimous that the United States must avoid any involvement in another European war. Americans, though, were shocked by the sweeping Nazi victories. Sensing the

> *Franklin Roosevelt is the best friend Britain ever had.*
> —WINSTON CHURCHILL

An articulate lawyer and businessman, Wendell Willkie (1892–1944) was an effective critic of the New Deal. Twice (1940 and 1944) the liberal Republican was nominated by his party to oppose FDR and twice he was defeated.

Roosevelt takes the salute from a contingent of "G.I. Joes" awaiting orders to go overseas in World War II as he reviews them from a jeep, a vehicle that some military experts regard as the greatest American mechanical contribution to World War II.

Using a take-off on his famous World War I army recruiting poster, artist James Montgomery Flagg (1877–1960) was pressed into service to use his popularity and skill to boost Roosevelt's campaign for a third term in 1940.

I WANT YOU F.D.R.

STAY AND FINISH THE JOB!

INDEPENDENT VOTERS' COMMITTEE OF THE ARTS *and* SCIENCES *for* ROOSEVELT

The royalists of the economic order have conceded that political freedom was the business of the Government, but they have maintained that economic slavery was nobody's business. . . . These economic royalists complain that we seek to overthrow the institutions of America. What they really complain of is that we seek to take away their power.

—FRANKLIN ROOSEVELT

divided mood of the country, Roosevelt tried to balance the desire to stay out of the war against the general inclination somehow to help the allies— England and France—defeat Germany. "Even a neutral," said Roosevelt, "cannot be asked to close his mind or his conscience."

Roosevelt urged Congress to repeal a ban instituted after World War I on sales of munitions to foreign countries. In its place the "cash-and-carry" programme came into force. It allowed belligerents to buy war material in the United States but only for cash, and the buyer had to carry away the material in their own ships. The law clearly favoured England and France as they controlled the major sea routes. Between September 1939 and August 1940, 44 per cent of all American exports went to the British Empire.

After several months of an inactive "sitting war", in the spring of 1940 the Germans conquered Denmark, Norway, Holland, Luxembourg, Belgium,

Isolationist sentiment was strong in America prior to Pearl Harbour. This advertisement in *The New York Times* drew charges that it was financed by German propaganda agents. New York congressman Hamilton Fish, Jr, an outspoken Roosevelt opponent who signed the ad, said that "not one cent" of its cost was paid for by German sources. He was right.

and France. Americans, numbed by the rapid German victories, rushed aid to besieged Great Britain. In September 1940 Roosevelt took a most daring step. By executive order, he exchanged 50 aged but usable destroyers with Great Britain for long-term leases to several British naval bases extending from Newfoundland to British Guiana (now named Guyana). Congress also passed the first peacetime draft in American history and voted to increase the nation's defences.

In the presidential election of 1940 Roosevelt broke the two-term presidential tradition and stood for an unprecedented third term. (The 22nd Amendment to the Constitution passed in 1951 now limits a president to two terms).

Three days after the German army entered Paris, Roosevelt made up his mind to seek reelection. To have decided not to stand again, he told Jim Farley "would have destroyed my effectiveness as the leader of the nation in the efforts of this country to cope with the terrible catastrophe raging in Europe." Roosevelt explained his break with the long-standing tradition to the Democratic convention:

"Lying awake. as I have on many nights, I have asked myself whether I have the right, as commander-in-chief of the army and navy, to call men and women to serve their country or to train themselves to serve, and, at the same time decline to serve my country in my own personal capacity, if I am called upon to do so by the people of my

Many in the crowd jeered when the aviator Charles A. Lindbergh (1902–1974) claimed in an Iowa speech in September 1941 that Jews and the Roosevelt administration were secretly conspiring to drive the United States into World War II. Lindbergh's increasingly anti-Semitic speeches angered and saddened many of his former admirers.

"Tora! Tora! Tora!" was the war cry of Japanese pilots as their bombs swept Pearl Harbour on 7 December 1941, destroying the might of the Pacific Fleet and catapulting the United States into World War II. The battleship *California* settles to the bottom of the sea, with other ships blazing astern of her.

country . . . Today, all private plans, all private lives, have been in a sense repealed by an overriding public danger. In the face of that public danger all those who can be of service to the Republic have no choice but to offer themselves for service in those capacities for which they may be fitted . . . I had made plans for myself, plans for a private life . . . but my conscience will not let me turn my back on a call to service."

Indeed, Roosevelt had made plans for his retirement to Hyde Park where he wanted to write his memoirs.

The Republicans nominated Wendell L. Willkie, a public utilities executive who gained national attention for his criticism of the Tennessee Valley Authority. Willkie accepted most of the New Deal legislation but derided the Roosevelt administration for its inefficiency and bureaucracy. Above all, he stressed the dangers of allowing one man to serve as president for twelve years. The main campaign issue was not foreign policy or national defence but the third term. Willkie lost to Roosevelt. (Roosevelt received 27,244,000 votes, Willkie 22,305,000.) Americans were willing to break with tradition and to endorse Franklin Roosevelt again.

Almost immediately the hard-fought New Deal domestic issues became obscured by the growing Nazi menace. By 1941 the United States had

Death and destruction ravage the air base at Hawaii's Hickam Field where U.S. planes were caught on the ground without warning. Japan's devastating attack on Pearl Harbour, America's naval outpost in the Pacific, immediately brought the U.S. into the war.

become, in Roosevelt's phrase, the "great arsenal of democracy". Through the Lend Lease Act, planes, tanks, and other articles of war were leased to Britain. The Chinese also received aid as they continued to oppose Japanese aggression in the Far East. (Total Lend Lease aid for the entire war amounted to $50 billion.) In June Roosevelt froze German and Italian credit in the United States, extending his ban to include Japan the following month. In August, during a meeting with British prime minister Winston Churchill, the two leaders issued the Atlantic Charter, which proclaimed "certain common principles" that would ensure "a better future for the world".

Then, on Sunday morning, 7 December 1941, Japenese naval aircraft forces bombed America's Pearl Habour naval base in Hawaii. While events had been indicating the possibility of confrontation with Japan for some time, this sudden attack stunned the nation. The following day, Congress passed a declaration of war against Japan. Similar resolutions were adopted on 11 December after

Four years of war took a heavy physical toll on FDR, and the strain showed as he spoke on his return from the Yalta Conference in 1945. To many of the president's critics, Yalta represented a pandering to the post-war interests of the Soviet Union, since Roosevelt had naively assumed that Soviet leader Joseph Stalin (1879–1953) would keep his promise to allow free elections in Soviet-occupied eastern Europe.

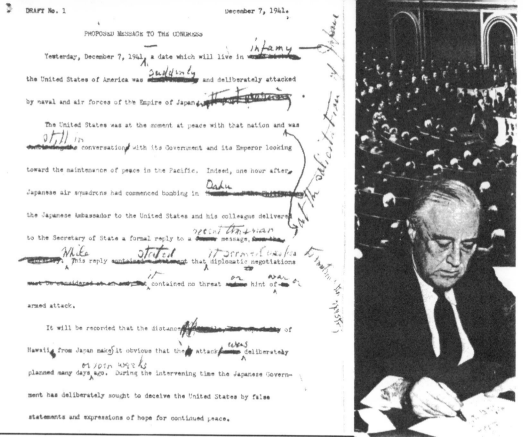

PROPOSED MESSAGE TO THE CONGRESS   December 7, 1941.

Yesterday, December 7, 1941, a date which will live in *infamy*

the United States of America was *suddenly* and deliberately attacked

by naval and air forces of the Empire of Japan.

The United States was at the moment at peace with that nation and was

still in conversation with its Government and its Emperor looking

toward the maintenance of peace in the Pacific. Indeed, one hour after

Japanese air squadrons had commenced bombing in *Oahu*

the Japanese Ambassador to the United States and his colleague delivered

to the Secretary of State a formal reply to a *recent American* message.

While This reply *stated* that diplomatic negotiations

it contained no threat *or* hint of *war or*

armed attack.

It will be recorded that the distance of

Hawaii from Japan makes it obvious that the attack *was* deliberately

or even weeks planned many days ago. During the intervening time the Japanese Govern-

ment has deliberately sought to deceive the United States by false

statements and expressions of hope for continued peace.

"A date which will live in infamy," begins the type-script of Roosevelt's address to Congress on 8 December 1941, reporting the Pearl Harbour attack and asking for a declaration of war on Japan. Similar declarations against Germany and Italy came three days later.

Germany and Italy declared war against the United States. America was now in the war—all the way.

World War II transformed Roosevelt into a global leader. While many domestic problems still remained unresolved, the president now had to devote almost all of his time and energy to winning the war. He assumed direction of the armed forces with the same determination that characterized his New Deal leadership. His first priority, obviously, was a military victory. The very democracy established by the Founding Fathers was at stake.

While American servicemen fought in Europe, Africa, and in Asia, as well as on the seven seas, civilians felt the war at home. They lived through the rationing of sugar, meat, coffee, petrol, and cigarettes. They performed regular air-raid drills. Unemployment all but disappeared as the civilian labour force swelled to a record 54.5 million. From July 1940 to August 1945, American factories and shipyards produced almost 300,000 aircraft; 86,000 tanks; 3,000,000 machine guns; 71,000 ships, plus more steel, oil, and aluminum than ever before in history. Even though taxes were increased to pay for the costs of these weapons and resources, the national debt at the end of the war had risen to $247 billion as compared to the pre-war $49 billion debt. The total monetary cost of this war to the United States was ten times the cost of World War I.

Several times during the war Roosevelt met the heads of the Allied governments to coordinate military efforts. Many of their decisions influenced the course of events after the war and in fact are still the subject of debate. At Casablanca in Morocco, in 1943, Roosevelt and Churchill declared that the Axis powers, including Germany, Japan, and Italy, must surrender without any conditions. This policy, explained the president, "does not mean the destruction of the population of Germany, Italy, and Japan, but it does mean the destruction of the philosophies in those countries which are based on conquest and the subjugation of other people." At Cairo in Egypt, later the same year, the two leaders promised Chiang Kai-shek, head of the Chinese Nationalist Government in China, that Manchuria and Formosa, then occupied by Japan, would be returned to China.

We may acknowledge that our enemies have performed a brilliant feat of deception, perfectly timed and executed with great skill. It was a thoroughly dishonourable deed, but we must face the fact modern warfare as conducted in the Nazi manner is a dirty business. We don't like it – we did not want to get in it – but we are in it, and we are going to fight it with everything we have got.
–FRANKLIN ROOSEVELT
speaking shortly after the Japanese attack on Pearl Harbour in 1941

As the country's interest was riveted on the imminence of war, Roosevelt found it proper to proclaim a "Bill of Rights Day", observing the 150th anniversary of the Constitution's first ten amendments. New York mayor Fiorello La Guardia looks on beside a poster listing FDR's own "Four Freedoms", which were meant to stand in marked contrast to the values of America's dictatorial enemies.

99

Military problems were discussed by the Big Three—Roosevelt, Churchill, and Joseph Stalin of the Soviet Union—at Teheran in Iran (1943), and again at Yalta in the Soviet Union (1945). The full text of the Yalta agreements, which dealt with disputes within Europe and Asia, and with the future of the United Nations, remained secret for two years. Critics have claimed that Roosevelt appeased the Soviet Union by agreeing to new boundaries for Poland as well as in Asia to the benefit of the Soviet Union. Others maintain that, in view of the military situation at the time, these decisions were necessary and realistic.

Gradually, the Japanese were beaten back in the Pacific. In Europe the Allied forces landed in North Africa and inched their way up through Sicily and Italy. On 6 June 1944—D-Day, perhaps the most critical day of the war—Allied forces directed by General Dwight D. Eisenhower invaded France. So began a series of Allied victories across France that led to the liberation of Paris on 25 August. On 7 March 1945, the Allies at last crossed the Rhine River and invaded Germany proper. On 7 May 1945, the Germans accepted unconditional surrender. The war in Europe had ended.

U.S. politics was not suspended during the war. In 1944 the Republicans nominated Governor Thomas E. Dewey of New York as their presidential candidate. The Republicans accepted most of Roosevelt's wartime direction and the president's commitment to a new international organization to prevent future wars. Dewey, instead, focused on the fourth term issue and on the president's health.

"All that is within me cries to go back to my home on the Hudson River," said Roosevelt, but if the people commanded it, he would serve again "like a good soldier". Roosevelt, now 62, was showing signs of extreme weariness. The dark circles under his eyes had become more pronounced, his hands quivered. Nevertheless, it was unthinkable that he should not be involved in finishing the war and making the peace. American voters, including soldiers who had cast their ballots on the battlefields, agreed. On 7 November 1944, some 48 million

German chancellor Adolf Hitler (1889–1945) addresses a Nazi rally in the 1930s. Like many Western leaders, Roosevelt mistakenly downplayed the significance of Hitler's rise to power.

Roosevelt, his lined face showing the strain of twelve years in the White House, first fighting the Depression and then assuming a major rle in the prosecution of World War II, delivers his fourth inaugural address on 10 January 1945. Within weeks the president would suffer a fatal stroke.

people voted and reelected Roosevelt by a majority of nearly 3.6 million votes and by 432 to 99 in the electoral vote. However, Roosevelt was to serve less than three months of his fourth term.

Throughout the war, every major decision was made by Franklin Roosevelt as he meticulously maintained the principle of civilian control. Controversy surrounds Roosevelt's wartime leadership, just as controversy surrounds almost every aspect of his presidency. One side portrays him as the gallant leader who rallied the free world to a great military victory which thrust the United States into the centre of the world stage. The other side presents a picture of a president whose errors in judgment led the United States into war and, once victorious, lost the peace to the Soviet Union at the Yalta Conference. Again, while we have numerous accounts of the war and of Roosevelt's wartime decisions, we lack Franklin Roosevelt's private version.

If we follow Roosevelt's speeches during 1944, we can see that he planned to continue the domestic New Deal reforms once the war ended. At the same time, he planned to work for democracy and democratic governments throughout the world. In an address to Congress in January 1944, he spoke of an economic Bill of Rights for all Americans:

> *I may say that I 'got along fine' with [Soviet leader] Marshal Stalin... and I believe that we are going to get along very well with him and the Russian people—very well indeed.*
> —FRANKLIN ROOSEVELT
> speaking in 1943, shortly after his return from a conference of Allied leaders at Teheran

—*The right to a useful and remunerative job:*
—*The right to earn enough to provide adequate food and clothing and recreation;*
—*The right of every farmer to raise and sell his products at a return which will give him and his family a decent living;*
—*The right of every businessman, large or small, to trade in an atmosphere free from unfair competition and domination by monopolies at home or abroad;*
—*The right of every family to a decent home;*
—*The right to adequate medical care;*
—*The right to adequate protection from the economic fears of old age, sickness, accident, and unemployment;*
—*The right to a good education;*
—*All these rights spell security . . . ;*
—*After the war is won, we must be prepared to move forward, in the implementation of these rights, to new goals of human happiness and well-being.*

Enrico Fermi (1901–1954), one of the "fathers" of the atomic bomb. Fermi first experimented with uranium in his native Italy in the early 1930s. He came to the United States in 1939 and headed a group at the University of Chicago which, in 1942, achieved the first self-sustaining nuclear chain reaction.

FDR and his successor, Harry Truman, shortly after the 1944 Democratic convention. It was one of the few times the two men were ever together.

Roosevelt the liberal had not forsaken the "forgotten man". The war was indeed a major interruption but, the president thought, the New Deal economy would return to its course once final military victory was obtained.

Roosevelt did not live to see the final victory over Germany and Japan nor the convening of the United Nations which he helped to create. On 12 April 1945, while resting at Warm Springs from his trip to Yalta, the president suffered a massive cerebral hemorrhage and died. He was 63 years old.

The word defeat was not in Franklin Rosevelt's vocabulary—neither in his personal life nor during the worst days of the Great Depression nor during the nation's most momentous war. On the contrary, Roosevelt symbolized hope—that the most formidable problem, the most formidable obstacle can be overcome. Indeed, perhaps hope is the lasting legacy of Franklin Roosevelt—hope for an improved life, hope for a better country, and hope for a peaceful world.

The New York Times.

LATE CITY EDITION

VOL. XCIV..No. 31,754.   NEW YORK, FRIDAY, APRIL 13, 1945.   THREE CENTS

PRESIDENT ROOSEVELT IS DEAD; TRUMAN TO CONTINUE POLICIES; 9TH CROSSES ELBE, NEARS BERLIN

U.S. AND RED ARMIES DRIVE TO MEET

Americans Across the Elbe in Strength Race Toward Russians Who Have Opened Offensive From Oder

WEIMAR TAKEN, RUHR POCKET SLASHED

Third Army Reported 19 Miles From Czechoslovak Border — British Drive Deeper in the North, Seizing Celle — Canadians Freeing Holland

OUR OKINAWA GUNS DOWN 118 PLANES

Japanese Fliers Start 'Suicide' Attacks on Fleet, Sink a Destroyer, Hit Other Ships

Army Leaders See Reich End at Hand

SECURITY PARLEY WON'T BE DELAYED

State Department Urges That World Be Shown We Plan No Changes in Policy

War News Summarized

FRIDAY, APRIL 13, 1945

Franklin Delano Roosevelt
1882-1945

END COMES SUDDENLY AT WARM SPRINGS

Even His Family Unaware of Condition as Cerebral Stroke Brings Death to Nation's Leader at 63

ALL CABINET MEMBERS TO KEEP POSTS

Funeral to Be at White House Tomorrow, With Burial at Hyde Park Home — Impact of News Tremendous

TRUMAN IS SWORN IN THE WHITE HOUSE

Members of Cabinet on Hand as Chief Justice Stone Administers the Oath

LAST WORDS: 'I HAVE TERRIFIC HEADACHE'

Roosevelt Was Posing for Artist When Hemorrhage Struck — He Died in Bedroom

Byrnes May Take Post With Truman

The New York Times announces the death of Roosevelt.

Colleagues, neighbours and
friends weep as FDR's body
leaves Warm Springs to the
tune of "Goin' Home",
played on a mouth organ.
The president, who com-
plained of "a massive
headache" while sitting for
his portrait in his cottage at
the polio spa, died there a
short time later.

Eleanor Roosevelt, whose
own career was to broaden
spectacularly as she became
a leading international
figure in politics, diplo-
macy, and even journalism,
pays her last respects to her
husband accompanied by
Anna Eleanor at the burial
of Franklin D. Roosevelt at
Hyde Park, 15 April 1945.

"All that is within me cries to go back to my home on
the Hudson River," Roosevelt said in 1944. Nine
months later, in April 1945, a distinguished cortege
followed his body to a simple burial service in the
rose garden of Hyde Park. In Washington, crowds
lined the streets as the coffin left the White House.

Chronology

30 January 1882	Born Franklin Delano Roosevelt at Springwood in Hyde Park, New York
1885–90	Tutored at home
	Journeys abroad with parents
1896-1900	Attends Groton School, Groton, Massachusetts
1900	Enters Harvard University
1901	Tours Europe with mother
	Reports for Harvard's *Crimson* magazine
1904	Graduates from Harvard
	Enters Columbia University Law School
17 March 1905	Marries Anna Eleanor Roosevelt
1910	Nominated and elected state senator from New York
1912	Reelected senator
1913	Appointed asistant secretary of the navy
	Resigns as state senator
4 Aug 1914	World War I officially begins when Britain joins Belgium, France, and Russia against Germany
1914–17	Supervises labour in navy yards
	Becomes interested in Caribbean affairs and visits Cuba and Santo Domingo
28 Feb 1917	The United States enters World War I
1919	Attends peace conference in Versailles in France
	Returns with Woodrow Wilson, who convinces him of the merits of the League of Nations
1920	Nominated as Democratic vice-presidential candidate with presidential running mate James M. Cox
August 1921	Struck with poliomyelitis
1928	Nominates Alfred E. Smith for president at Democratic convention in Houston, Texas
	Elected governor of New York
29 October 1929	Stock market crash in New York signals beginning of worldwide economic depression
1930	Reelected governor of New York
	Nominated Democratic presidential candidate to run against Herbert Hoover
1932	Elected president, winning 472 out of 531 electoral votes
1933–36	Implementation of Roosevelt's New Deal programmes provides gradual economic recovery
3 Nov 1936	Reelected president, defeating Alfred M. Landon
1936–40	Faces increasing restrictions on his executive powers as federal district judges and Supreme Court judges declare vital parts of New Deal unconstitutional

5 Nov 1940	Reelected to third presidential term, defeating Wendell Willkie
7 Dec 1941	Japanese attack Pearl Harbour The United States enters World War II
Nov 1943	Meets Soviet leader Joseph Stalin at Teheran Conference
6 June 1944	Allied forces invade Europe (D-Day)
Nov 1944	Reelected to an unprecendented fourth term as president
February 1945	Attends Yalta Conference with Joseph Stalin and British premier Winston Churchill
12 April 1945	Dies, aged 63, at Warm Springs, Georgia

Further Reading

Burns, James MacGregor. *Roosevelt: The Lion and the Fox.* New York: Harcourt, Brace and World, 1958.

——. *Roosevelt: The Soldier of Freedom.* New York: Harcourt, Brace and World, 1970.

Einaudi, Mario. *The Roosevelt Revolution.* London: Greenwood Press, 1977.

Hassett, William D. *Off the Record with Franklin Delano Roosevelt.* London: Greenwood Press, 1958.

Larrabee, Eric. *Commander in Chief: Franklin Delano Roosevelt, His Lieutenants and Their War.* London: Andre Deutsch, 1987.

Morgan, Ted. *Franklin Delano Roosevelt: A Biography.* London: Grafton Books, 1986.

Romasco, Albert U. *Roosevelt's New Deal: Politics of Recovery.* New York: Oxford University Press, 1983.

Traynor, J. *Roosevelt's America, 1932–41.* London: Macmillan, 1987.

Index